PRAISE FOR *STRATEGIC HUMAN RESOURCE MANAGEMENT*

"This is a must-read book, whether you are an experienced HR professional or a novice. It is an indispensable guide to understanding the world of work and adding strategic value by challenging you to rethink your understanding of HR. The future is really is all about the People Experience and awareness of self, business, industry and profession."
Shakil Butt, HR Hero, HR and leadership consultant

"This much-needed and easy-to-read book provides a fantastic guide for today's HR professional. It is a great combination of education in modern practice and terminology blended with practical advice and encouragement for how to navigate the shifting commercial landscapes that we all face."
Kim Atherton, Chief People Officer, OVO Energy, and CEO, Just3Things

"Finally, a professional self-help book for HR practitioners from the Bouncebackability Queen herself! It provides a highly practical, real-world look at what it means to lead people strategy across organizations, starting with what it means to lead yourself. As an avid fan of Karen's PX vision, I look forward to a future HR profession full of human-centric and business-focused practitioners, closely collaborating with their people and leaders to build commercially successful and sustainable organisations. As Karen says, 'To be inspirational, you must first be inspired,' and this book will do that for you."
Natal Dank, Chief HR Agilist, Southern Blue Consulting, and co-founder, Agile HR Community

"In a world where HR has to be as creative, agile and future-focused as any other part of the business, this book shows not only how important this is but how to make it possible. It draws upon real experiences from the front line of HR, tackles modern issues and offers insights into the mindset of a successful HR practitioner. It will be the go-to resource for all my HR coachees who are looking to make their mark in business."
Paul Deeprose, Founder of The Career Gym

"This book is a massive gift not just to HR leaders but to all leaders. Karen turns fundamental concepts into extremely practical steps but most of all she conveys all of her experiences and recommendations in a truly human way. After reading this book you will look after yourself and your people differently and you will be totally confident that you are adding additional value to your organisation."
David Frost, Organizational Development Director, Total Produce

"An excellent handbook for anyone with HR or line management responsibilities, putting the employee experience at the forefront. The chapters are well researched, providing snackable information with sections on how your thinking will be changed, toolkit essentials and reflection questions."
Julie Merritt, General Manager

"This is an inspirational guide written by a 'been there, seen it, done it' industry specialist who knows what she is talking about and is not afraid to explain it. By learning about staff, the benefits of a personal network, the industry you work in and your aspirations, the reader can grow into a passionate leader and guide a business to become a driving force in their field."
Stu Walker, Managing Director, Integrated Sales & Marketing Solutions

Strategic Human Resource Management

An HR professional's toolkit

Karen Beaven

KoganPage

First published in Great Britain and the United States in 2019 by Kogan Page Limited

2nd Floor, 45 Gee Street	c/o Martin P Hill Consulting	4737/23 Ansari Road
London	122 W 27th Street	Daryaganj
EC1V 3RS	New York, NY 10001	New Delhi 110002
United Kingdom	USA	India

© Karen Beaven 2019

The right of Karen Beaven to be identified as the author of this work has been asserted by her in accordance with the Copyright, Designs and Patents Act 1988.

ISBNs

Hardback	978 0 7494 9796 5
Paperback	978 0 7494 8404 0
eBook	978 0 7494 8405 7

British Library Cataloguing-in-Publication Data

A CIP record for this book is available from the British Library.

Library of Congress Cataloging-in-Publication Data

A CIP record for this book is available from the Library of Congress.

Typeset by Integra Software Services, Pondicherry
Print production managed by Jellyfish
Printed and bound in Great Britain by CPI Group (UK) Ltd, Croydon CR0 4YY

To my beautiful daughter Aurora and my wonderful family, whose unconditional support, patience and love I am eternally grateful for.

XXX

CONTENTS

ABOUT THE AUTHOR

Karen Beaven is a multi-award-winning HR Director who is accredited at Chartered FCIPD level. In 2015 she was awarded the accolade of HR Director of the Year at the HR Excellence Awards in addition to picking up awards for Best HR Team, Most Effective Recruitment Strategy and the overall HR Excellence Gold Award. In addition, Karen has frequently appeared in the HR Most Influential rankings and has also been recognized as a Global HR Superstar by *HRO Today* magazine.

Karen began her career outside of the HR profession and spent time working as a horse-riding instructor before moving across into retail and progressing up the ranks into a retail management position. From this experience Karen then moved into her first HR role and built her career, working with prestigious brands such as Sainsburys, HMV, The Arcadia Group, AllSaints and River Island.

During her time at River Island, and in addition to her HR remit, Karen also founded a professional styling service for the brand. This service, known as 'Style Studio', now operates in a number of key flagship locations and is a reflection of what can be achieved with Karen's entrepreneurial and commercial approach to HR.

Karen now runs her own company, PX Innovations Ltd, through which she provides coaching and consultancy services in addition to operating a membership platform for progressive HR practitioners – The HR Entrepreneur's Network. Karen also operates the 'PX Innovation Hub', a free Facebook group for people working in HR and associated professions.

In her own business Karen has a particular focus on supporting individuals in the areas of delivering commercial results, self-care and mental wellbeing and with matters surrounding identity, perception and personal brand. Karen also supports organizations that wish to adopt a more progressive approach to HR and switch to a 'People Experience (PX)' delivery model.

www.karenbeaven.com

ACKNOWLEDGEMENTS

It's fair to say that this has not been an easy book to write for a number of reasons, not least that in the year I decided to write it I was also on a journey of recovery from a personal breakdown which rather abruptly disrupted my career and life. There were so many times that it would have been easy to quit and say I couldn't do it, and so many times where I was at the point of that, but I was fortunate enough to have people around me who didn't give up on me and who helped me through. Therefore in writing these acknowledgements I feel gratitude and thanks on so many levels it's hard to really articulate the scale of it.

First, I want to thank my amazing parents who have supported me in every crazy endeavour I have ever taken up in my life, mostly without question, always encouraging me to do the things that make me happy and to embrace life. They are the most wonderful people who always know just what to say, what I need to hear, and who are always there with love and support exactly when I need it. You are smart and gracious people who are both an inspiration to me and I really don't have the words to thank you enough for the confidence you have given me and the life you have enabled me to live. I also want to thank my brother, who probably played a key role in developing my competitive nature, for supporting me without judgement as my career progressed. Love you bro!

Next, I want to thank my awesome husband Dom and our beautiful daughter Aurora for bringing sunshine into my life and inspiring me to keep going even when the going got tough. I have a feeling I'm not a particularly easy person to live with 24/7 but you guys seem to navigate this and uplift me, motivate me and drive me to be a better person every day. Thanks so much for your support.

I'd like to thank my phenomenal business mentor Sháá Wasmund MBE, who came into my life at exactly the right moment and without whom this book probably wouldn't have been written. Thanks also to Team Sháá – Shari D Teigman, Matt Thomas, Andy Moss and Chris Wharton – who all helped make a difficult year a little bit easier.

Thanks to Tea Colaianni, a wonderful mentor who has inspired and motivated me through exceptional circumstances, always providing encouragement and the voice of reason.

I'd like to thank the following superstars who kindly contributed to this book. You are all wonderful humans whose support I am incredibly thankful for: Sián Harrington, Nebel Crowhurst, Janine Jenkinson, Katie Jacobs, Caspar Craven, Simon Hedaux, Tom Ormond, Sam Allen, Orlando Martins, Katrina Collier, Keith Budden, Andy Spence, Nalin Miglani.

A special thank you to the wonderful Emma Taylor who motivated me, supported me and generally was there, helping me in whatever way she could whenever she could, including hugs with her amazing horse Rchi, so thanks to Rchi too!

Also special thanks to Farida Kaikobad whose support, encouragement and kindness will forever be an inspiration to me.

Finally, a shout out and thanks to some more superstars who inspire me and who have supported me in writing this book, perhaps in ways that they didn't even realize. You're all awesome! Thanks so much to Eugenio Pirri, Perry Timms, Mandy Coalter, Jabbar Sardar, Louise Winstanley, Kim Burton, Clare Hems, Marina Olvera, Deborah Owens, my HR team at River Island – still love you guys. Barry Flack, Shakil Butt, Nick Holley, Natal Dank, Rob Briner, Nikki Thomas, Garry Turner, Andy Dodman, Lucy Dodd, Mervyn Dinnen, Michelle Harte, Harveen Gill, Jo Bickley, Giles Farnham, Charlotte Hallaways, Naomi Dominique, Wendy Cartwright, Angela O'Connor, Cris Beswick, Jo-Anne Karlsson and of course the wonderful team at Kogan Page who helped make all of this possible; special thanks to Lucy Carter and Stephen Dunnell.

PREFACE

The reinvention of HR

There has never been a more exciting and challenging time to work in HR. It would be easy to say that we are on the cusp of reinvention or transformation but the truth is we are already in the thick it. Transformation is all around us and however we feel about it we are all active participants in this journey. It's my belief that we are moving towards a point of co-creation and co-ownership of HR activity and by this I mean that the traditional barriers that we may have associated as being between HR's remit and an operational management remit are falling away. This is being enabled in many ways by advancements in technology that deliver data and functionality directly into the hands of an end user without the need for lengthy admin processes and third-party (HR) intervention. All of this builds the perfect platform for delivery of 'People Experience', which we will explore as part of this book.

Time to push the reset button

I propose that it's time to push the reset button for the HR profession. It's never too late to reboot professionally, especially so where roles within HR and the expectation of delivery are changing and at an unprecedented pace. For this reason, it is vitally important for individuals who work within HR and in associated professions to take their own development and learning seriously. This applies at all levels from entry level all the way up to the lead Chief People Officer position and applies equally regardless of how long you have worked within the profession. My recommendation is that this learning and reset be structured in such a way that it encompasses the four key areas below:

- self-awareness;
- business awareness;
- industry awareness;
- profession awareness.

This then provides a robust platform from where skills and practices can be developed that support enhanced delivery of commercial results, improved self-care and mental wellbeing for the HR professional, and an improved perception of personal brand linked to professional competence.

A model for People Experience

People are sick of HR getting in the way and of organizations that talk about 'the future of work' but where, as an employee, you're stuck with the equivalent of 'Windows 98' and a line manager who needs you to confirm to a working style or hours that suit them but which don't allow the individual to flourish. Can you imagine in your organization if external customers were treated in the same way that you treat your employees, with the same level of services and products? Would you feel comfortable with that? Would you have any customers left? It's an interesting perspective and one which inspired me to consider a model for People Experience (PX) which I'm delighted to share with you and which may go some way to address this but only when combined with a common-sense approach and an attitude from leaders and managers which clearly puts 'People' not 'Product' first.

Support

Everyone needs support from time to time and through this book, my HR Entrepreneur's Network and my wider work I aim to provide that for all people working in HR and any professions associated with it. This book is also perfect for business leaders, CEOs and operational managers who wish to improve their results and understand how HR/PX can be delivered to best effect.

Through the experiences I have had I have become incredibly passionate about supporting individuals working within the profession and also in supporting organizations who want to enhance the working experience for their employees and through this improve their commercial results. I know it's not always easy, in fact HR and leading people can be incredibly hard, and that's what influenced my decision to position elements of this book as a toolkit that can be dipped into when needed, with prompts for action to help embed learning.

The book is written from a very practical perspective which I hope makes it accessible for anyone who chooses to read it. It reflects my personal experiences and viewpoints associated with the highs and lows of working in HR.

We are all capable of owning and shaping our profession and we are all capable of improving our commercial and personal results and our level of self-care. All we need to do is to take one small step and then keep going. Work to be the best version of you, do work you love with people who inspire you, and all the rest will slowly start to fall into place. Your career is not a sprint, it's a fascinating journey, so take time to enjoy it, help others along the way and consider not only the experiences you create for the people around you but also – and perhaps most importantly – consider the experiences you create for yourself and how those experiences enrich and improve the quality of your own life.

You've got this!

Introduction

This book is a practical text which promotes the concept of 'People Experience' – PX – as an alternative to traditional 'Human Resources'. It explores the strategic contribution of the function and explores how HR can support overall business goals whilst still maintaining a focus on developing and engaging individual employees through deployment of a PX model.

The book is split into four sections and promotes learning and discovery through the key components of knowing yourself, knowing your business, knowing your industry and knowing your profession.

Knowing yourself. We start with a focus on knowing yourself and position this as the foundation which will enable you to operate at a strategic level within the HR profession. It can be a valuable exercise to conduct a deep dive into our own soft skills and the factors which can impact on our performance. We pay particular attention to the concept of self-care and the unique challenges a career in HR can place on this.

Knowing your business. Here we move on to look at the importance of really getting to know the details of how the business you work in operates. We look at how you can then move on to leverage this knowledge to enhance your profile within your business and the results you can achieve in your role.

Knowing your industry. In this section we broaden our focus to encompass the industry you operate in and consider what influence this has on both the performance of your organization and your own career development. We consider how you can stretch your impact beyond the remit of your current organization and make lasting change at industry level.

Knowing your profession. Finally we promote the importance of fully understanding your profession and professional responsibilities in addition to looking at factors shaping the profession for the future. We consider how you can make an impact within your profession and also encourage you to consider how you can play an active role in shaping the profession for the future.

So why a toolkit? Let's look at the definition as a starting point.

Toolkit

1 A set of tools designed to be used together or for a particular purpose.

2 Software designed to perform a specific function, esp. to solve a problem.

(Collinsdictionary.com, 2018)

Therefore, it is my hope that through reading this book you'll find ways to add to your own toolkit, ditch the tools that aren't working for you any more and find some new ones to help enhance the work you do going forward.

Activity 1: Knowledge and impact

Before we get started I want you to take a moment to consider the four-box grid below. The headings are fairly self-explanatory; however, for clarity consider them as follows.

Yourself. In this section, think about all of the elements that enable you to operate as the best version of yourself: your motivations, ambitions, goals, your mental and physical wellbeing. Also think about any stress points, areas for development and emotional triggers.

Your business. In this section, think about the business you currently work for, or the one you aspire to work for if you're looking to secure employment there sometime soon.

Your industry. Here we're talking about the industry in which your current or desired business operates, eg retail, leisure, oil and gas.

Your profession. Your chosen occupation, and I'm going to take a guess that if you're reading this book there's a good chance it's Human Resources, although as you will establish as we progress through this book I'm encouraging you to think more along the lines of 'People Experience' or 'PX' as a description for the work we do. Equally, this model and text applies if your profession could also be defined as 'General Management' or business leadership, as you will also discover that my vision for PX and the future of our profession promotes a broadened accountability that should be shared across a leadership team for maximum benefit, as opposed to sitting with one function.

What I'd like you to do is to draw out the basic four boxes for yourself and as you will see I have added the title 'Knowledge' to this first table. I'd like you to shade out an additional square within the box as an indicator of your current knowledge level in this area. For example, if you feel that at the present time your current knowledge of your profession is greater than your knowledge of the business you work in, the square you have shaded in the 'Profession' box should be larger than the square you have shaded in the 'Business' box.

There's going to be all kinds of reasons for how you size your boxes at the present time so make a note of any that come up as you complete the exercise and also date the sheet you do this on too as it's going to be a useful marker for your progress and to determine where and how to focus your time and energy.

Figure 0.1   Knowledge map

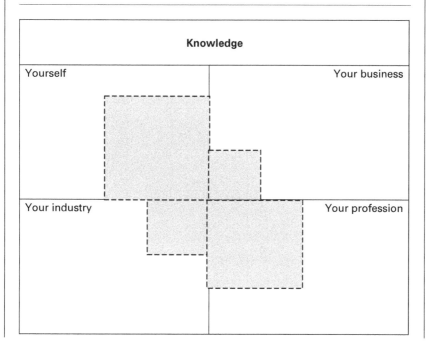

Next, we're going to repeat the activity but this time I want you to consider your current 'Impact' in each of the sections. For example, how visible are you and how valuable is the impact you make in each area? You need to be really honest with yourself here, especially when it comes to thinking about the impact you have within your business. Think in commercial terms: what have you delivered or enabled someone else to deliver that has really made a difference?

In terms of 'yourself', when you think about impact, think about self-care. What impact are your current life and career choices having on your ability to show up, deliver great work and be an all-round awesome human? The higher the level of self-care, the bigger the box!

Again, make some notes about the reasons for your sizing of the squares and ensure you date the document so you have a measure you can refer back to.

When you've completed the activity I want you to be brave and get a second opinion. Find someone whose opinion you trust and ask them to complete the same activity based on how they perceive your knowledge and impact. Give them the form template and ask them to make a few notes on why they have chosen to size the squares in the way they have. You can

Figure 0.2   Impact map

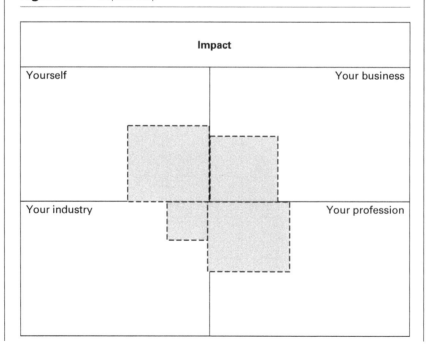

then cross-reference your perception with theirs and then, taking onboard their feedback, consider what this means for your personal development planning. Make a list of any development areas that have been highlighted for you and then rank them in priority order in terms of impact. Take the top three from the list as action points to get started on immediately and (for the moment) ditch the rest!

By completing this activity you should now have a good idea of your priority areas of development so feel free to skip ahead and jump right into the section and chapters of this text that support your learning in these areas. Of course, you're welcome to read this text cover to cover and I sincerely hope you do. I also know that if you're like me you want results *fast* and as such I wholeheartedly support you skipping ahead and dipping into the info that meets your immediate needs in the moment

Reference

Collinsdictionary.com (2018) Toolkit definition and meaning, available at: www.collinsdictionary.com/dictionary/english/toolkit [accessed 17 October 2018]

PART ONE
Know yourself

Continuous personal development 01

Introduction

In this chapter we look to explore the importance of ongoing and meaningful personal development activities for individuals working within Human Resources. We will identify some vital components to include within your own personal development strategy and suggest some tools you may wish to sharpen up or deploy in order to accelerate your learning and career. With development planning being such an intrinsic element of most HR roles it's not only important to role model great practices here, it's also essential if you hope to remain current and credible in the environment within which you operate.

How will this chapter shape my thinking?

- It will encourage you to clarify the 'purpose' behind your plan and ensure that activities you undertake are meaningful and supportive of that core purpose.
- It will provide you with a framework for your own personal development which incorporates elements of Agile project management.
- It will promote the importance of accountability in development planning and establish models through which this can be delivered.

Purpose

I think of myself as a serial learner. Seriously, I can't switch off this drive for knowledge and even if I could I don't think I'd want to. This is something you need to take very seriously if you want to make a real impact in your career. You need to own it!

I know, maybe you got this far without a plan, right? Maybe you did, but what you'll never know is how much further you could have got and how much more you could have achieved if you'd taken time to map things out and apply a little more focus to setting and achieving stretching goals and targets for yourself. Also, think of this as a reflection of how you view business development too; you wouldn't run a multimillion-dollar business without a plan, so why would it be ok to run your career and life without one? Trust me, it's worth investing in yourself here and taking some time out to create the action plan that's going to enable you to achieve your potential.

People often suggest that successful development planning starts with some basic goal setting; I'm going to take a step back from there and encourage you to think instead about the *purpose* for your plan as the very first point. You need to be clear on *why* you are doing something for it to be truly meaningful and you need it to be meaningful if it's going to be effective. When you go back to think about your 'why', think of it as a process of discovery, not invention (Sinek, 2009). By that I mean I encourage you to remain connected to your own identity and be authentic in what you set out to achieve. To move forwards it's important to reflect on the past and ensure we are pursuing a career that we want because we want to and not because someone is pushing us into it or because we have a mistaken belief that it's the only path available to us.

Goal setting

To get going here, think about setting some short-, mid- and long-terms goals; you define the timespans so that they are meaningful and relevant for you. It can be useful to articulate your goals in a specific way in order to be clear with yourself about why that goal matters to you. Why this goal, why now and what will it give you? Think about how your goals link to your personal and professional strategy, and consider this: 'A winning strategy combines analytically sound, ambitious but logical goals with methods that help people experience new, often very ambitious goals, as exciting, meaningful and uplifting – creating a deeply felt determination to move, make it happen, and win, now' (Kotter, 2008).

A common test that most will be familiar with for goal setting utilizes the 'SMART' model, which asks, is this goal specific, measurable, achievable, realistic and time bound? I also take inspiration from the world of Kanban in formulating mine. For example, instead of formulating the goal as per example one or example two below, I add a little more depth to shape it in the format of example three.

Example One: Starting goal

- Learn how to use webinar technology.

Example Two: SMART goal

- Specific: I'd like to learn how to use Zoom (other providers are available) webinar technology and ensure that 40 per cent of employees access my webinar.
- Measurable: I'll know I've completed it when I have delivered my first webinar.
- Achievable: Yes, it seems pretty straightforward and info on how to do it is readily available.
- Realistic: Yes, I know other people who are less tech-savvy than me who run webinars.
- Time bound: Within three months.

Example Three: Kanban/user story goal

- As a human resources director, I would like to deliver a webinar on the subject of personal development planning within my business so that more people can access information to enhance their careers and learn skills to help them drive the business more quickly at a time and place that suits them.
- My acceptance criteria for this will be that the webinar will be delivered within three months and 40 per cent of employees will access it.

When you have your goals, write them down and keep them somewhere you can see them. Then consider how you might add a 'stretch' goal into the mix if there isn't one there already. Something that's going to take you beyond your comfort zone and accelerate your progress. It's important to remember that every activity you put on your development plan should take you a step closer to achieving your ambitions so be sure you're being brave enough here in order to keep yourself on track.

Something to consider adding to your toolkit here is a physical or virtual planning journal to help you keep track of and manage your goals. Trello is a good starting point if you're looking for a digital option but with the pace of transformation in this arena a quick Google search will bring up many other solutions for you to investigate. If you're looking to build pace and momentum with your development activity it can be useful to work in 90-day blocks as a maximum to ensure you have the clarity of focus needed to gain traction. This method should add value to longer-term goal setting as opposed to replacing it completely. Within the 90-day plan you can then break down your development activity further into realistic timescales that keep you motivated at the appropriate level without layering on any undue stress and pressure. Consider two- or four-week 'sprints' to achieve set objectives within your development plan.

Going Agile

Personally, I bring in elements from Agile software development to my plans; it works for me but you really need to try out a few styles to find the approach that's best for you. The Agile Alliance defines Agile as 'The ability to create and respond to change in order to succeed in an uncertain and turbulent environment' (Agile Alliance, 2018). Essentially, Agile is a way of working that combines a number of set routines and practices with the end result of delivering more useable work, more quickly in an organizational context. In relation to personal development planning I find it useful to take inspiration from this methodology both in terms of my own practice and also when I'm working with other people. Table 1.1 shows an example of the template I use to structure an Agile Development plan.

I'm also going to let you in on another secret to creating an effective development plan: the secret is to limit the amount of activity you have going on at any one moment. Again, this takes inspiration from the world of Agile and Kanban; you need to limit your work in progress if you want to get things done. The way to do this is to create a backlog of activities that you want to take on, and next to remove any that don't take you a step closer to your established goals. This narrows down your focus to the things that really matter; then prioritize the remaining activities in order of importance. This is the list that would be added to the first column in Table 1.1.

Next, from your backlog, select three activities to move into the 'discovery' phase, explore these options in turn, and then if after further research you still believe it's the right course of action move it into an 'in progress' column. Again, limit yourself to only having three things live at any one time. Don't worry – as soon as it's done (meeting your acceptance criteria for 'done') you can move it on to the next column and take on another one into the 'in progress' phase. By managing your development activity in this way, you stand a better chance of ensuring your focus and effort are directed in the right way and stand a greater chance of success in achieving your goals.

You'll also note in the template there is a column that is headed 'blocked'. This is where the activities move to if they are stalled or blocked beyond your control. For example, maybe you've identified a development activity that requires you to attend a training course, you researched options for it in the 'discovery' phase, then went on to book a place on the course in the 'in progress' phase but now you need to wait five months before the course starts. At this stage you haven't completed the activity but there's also nothing further you can do to move it on at the moment either. Therefore, it now sits in the 'blocked' column until the course begins. When it begins it moves to the second 'in progress' column before finishing in 'done' when it has been completed.

In addition to my plan, I also have a vision board to feed my creative soul. It's an A1 board with images, motivational quotes and ambitions on it. This can be a great option if you've tried multiple

Table 1.1 Agile development plan

	Backlog of activities	Activities in discovery phase	Activities in progress	Blocked	In progress	Done
Example action	Read *Transformational HR* book.	Investigate options for org design qualification.	Agile HR training.	Leadership development programme (next intake in 9 months).	Read *Tribe of Mentors* book.	Attend CIPD conference.

variations of text-led plans in the past and they haven't worked for you. It's simple enough to put together and you can use any images that resonate with you. Someone I know has a picture of their dream car on theirs next to the date they want to own it by. I see mine every day and it reminds me what all the hard work is for. If you're more of a visual person, give it a go and see how it works out for you.

Accountability

There is no one better placed in this world to drive your personal development than you. It seems like a simple thing but I've lost count of the amount of conversations I've had with people where they've been happy to hand over their own personal development to someone else or to 'fate' and then complain that no one has ever helped them or *made* them do it. They explain that the reason their career hasn't progressed is because no one gave them a development plan and they carry a sincere perception of injustice and resentment because of this. Now, I'm all for helping people who want to progress but we can't own anyone else's development or responsibility for it any more than we can (or would want to) own any other element of their personality. Self-development starts with yourself so if you want a development plan, you need to motivate yourself to create it and be accountable for it. So, When you're talking to people about your plan you need to be coming from the angle of creating tangible *results* from it and talking about those, not talking about *excuses* for not having it and for not delivering results here.

Another common thing I encounter is people who commit to create their own development plan as part of a coaching or mentoring programme, then guess what? They never do it. Don't be that person; if you commit to do something, do it! It's in your interest to do the work. It doesn't matter what format it's in, the only important thing is it works for you and gives you the type of goals and motivation you need to achieve the things you set out to achieve.

So, it's your responsibility to do the work, but it does also help to have someone you can call on as an accountability partner from time to time. There are a couple of ways you can do this. Either set up something informal with someone you already know and trust, or sign up to work with an experienced coach or mentor who can support you with this in a professional capacity. Also, look for social media groups that encourage this as part of their community.

Reflection

It's also important to remember the value of reflection and allowing time and space for the learning to sink in. If you are a planner, plan in some time to rest, and have some points where you take a bit of time out to consolidate what you already know. It can feel frustrating at times but trust me, your mental health will thank you for it in the long term.

Conclusion

We're fortunate to live in a time where the sources of personal development material are abundant. There really are no limits on options so have fun and explore which works best for you. Whether you choose books, journals, newspapers, podcasts or blogs, there's really no excuses for not getting started today.

There are multiple options for how to structure and plan your development activity and no right or wrong approaches as long as your method passes the 'results not excuses' test.

As we now live in a time where it will be the norm for people to work into their 70s and 80s (Gratton and Scott, 2016) the implications of this on the need for continuous personal development are profound, particularly when viewed in the context of the changing world of work and accelerated advancements in technology. For example, imagine a scenario where an organization chose not to investigate trends and developments around artificial intelligence – that would be unheard of for most commercial operations. However, in context very few individuals will be looking at this in terms of what it might mean for their own personal development and what the arrival or mainstream AI might mean for the way they work in the future. It's not beyond reason to expect that at some point we will all become 'managers' of AI agents in some capacity and that this will be the norm and expected. Learning how to best utilize digital technology now and incorporating this into your development plan will ensure you are better placed to remain current and be progressive throughout the duration of your career, even if it spans into your 80s. Investment in CPD activities for employees will also become a determining factor in the success of organizations in light of these factors and even now businesses are reaping the rewards from supporting the personal development of the individuals working within them. There is no better time to start and no better time to prioritize your own development in order that you can advance your career and help others as they seek to develop theirs.

Toolkit essentials: 10 steps to successful personal development

1 Define the purpose of your development plan and consider the timeframe for it.

2 Own it! Accept that the best person to be responsible for your development is you.

3 Ask for help or a second opinion when you need it.

4 Set goals and stretch goals that link in to your purpose. Be clear on your definition of 'done' for these goals.

5 Choose development activities that suit your personal learning style.

6 Limit your work in progress, and only actively work on a maximum of three things at once.

7 Create a vision board to remind you what you're working towards.

8 Find an appropriate accountability partner, mentor or group.

9 Factor in time for reflection on learning and for rest in your planning process.

10 Start today!

Questions for reflection

Q. If you could only work on three development activities at this moment in time, which three would you choose?

Q. How do these three development activities compare to the ones you created in Activity 1?

Q. Can you define in one sentence the purpose of your current development plan?

Q. Have you clearly articulated your goals for the next 30, 60 and 90 days?

Q. Who is your accountability partner for your development activity?

References

Agile Alliance (2018) *Agile 101*, available from: www.agilealliance.org/agile101/ [accessed 19 January 2018]

Gratton L, and Scott, A (2016) *The 100 Year Life: Living and working in an age of longevity*, Bloomsbury, London

Kotter, J (2008) *A Sense of Urgency*, Harvard Business School Press

Sinek, S (2009) *Start With Why: How great leaders inspire everyone to take action*, Penguin, London

Drive and passion

Introduction

Like many people, I didn't explicitly choose HR as a profession; I chose to do work I loved with people who inspired me. It just so happened that HR is where I found my home. Eighteen years in it's now safe to say I chose HR and I'm passionate about this profession and helping people build their careers within it.

In his book *Drive*, Daniel H Pink puts forward that we are driven by three essential things: autonomy – the freedom to direct our lives, mastery – the desire to achieve excellence in what we do, and purpose – the knowledge that what we do is in service of something bigger than ourselves. Together these elements combine to form the compelling force that drives us and determines how we shape our lives. I add passion to the mix as the key component that sets our souls on fire and makes us come alive. Regard passion as a key element of your individuality and a defining factor of your personal USP. Throughout my career (and life) I've been led very much by my passion and have made purposeful career choices in order to enable me to throw my heart and soul into my work. Perhaps a little too much on some occasions!

In this chapter we look at how we can channel our drive and passion to maximum effect throughout our careers.

How will this chapter shape my thinking?

- It will encourage you to identify your true passion and leverage that as part of your personal Unique Selling Proposition (USP).
- It will support you in identifying and removing blocks that may be having an impact on your current levels of motivation and drive.
- It will encourage you to develop mechanisms for bouncebackability and to deploy them readily when the need arises.

Passion

Lombardo and Eichinger (2009) highlight tapping into your passion as the solution to a scenario where you might otherwise blend into the crowd. They encourage the reader to identify their passion and appoint themselves as champion for it. The outcome of that is that as an individual you begin to develop your personal brand and reputation, and naturally others who share that same passion or who require it in their organizations are drawn towards you. This is an important thing to consider if the market for your particular skill set is crowded, or if you're up against stiff competition for your dream job and you need to leverage competitive edge.

In 2016, Alaina Love, President of Purpose Linked Consulting, surveyed 3,500 individuals on the topic of passion. Her firm's research 'has revealed that purpose and passion are integrally linked, like the two strands of DNA that comprise the code for life'. As Alaina explained, 'Passion is, therefore, better defined as the outward expression of one's inner purpose. It's the energy that can be tapped to accomplish deeper life goals.' So, if we take this in the context of the previous chapter, consider your passion as the energy that will fuel the activities you have set out to achieve as part of your personal development.

Activity 2: Your unique selling proposition (USP)

According to *Entrepreneur* magazine, USP is defined as 'The factor or consideration presented by a seller as the reason that one product or service is different from and better than that of the competition.' If we reframe that to define what that might mean from a personal perspective, we get the following: 'The factor or consideration presented by an individual as the reason that their product or service is different from and better than that of the competition.' Something to consider, as after all, even those who are permanently employed can be considered to be providing a 'service' of some form to the organization that employs them.

Take some time now to create your personal USP statement, ensuring that this conveys your authentic passion. Limit this to an elevator pitch format. Test it out on someone who knows you well for a preliminary validity check, then utilize it at the next professional networking event you attend. Use the questions below to help shape your thinking.

- What is the service that you currently provide to your employer and/or clients? Can you define it in one sentence?
- How do you measure how satisfied your customer (employer) is with the service you currently provide?
- What makes the way you deliver the service you provide different to the way that someone else might do the job?

Remember, if you want to stand out from the crowd you need to tap into your passion in order to create a movement, build a client base and set yourself out as having a unique proposition that gives you an edge over your competitors.

Identifying blockers

Not only do you need passion to drive your own development, it also takes a lot of passion to drive the HR function in any business, particularly if you intend to do this in a progressive and connected way. HR directors share a responsibility to innovate, create and drive developments within our field, promoting quality and excellence in all organizational areas and forging forwards as true business leaders who just happen to have the letters 'HR' in their job titles. To support this, it's interesting to look at a feature from the *Deloitte HR Times* blog from November 2017, where the headline was, 'A true HR strategy is about more than HR'. The authors suggest that we should consider the following: 'Imagine HR "playing up" a level and transitioning from a support function that offers "HR" advice and guidance to business leaders, to operating as a co-owner, enabler, and influencer of the business strategy and operations' (Mazor, Sobey and Kunkleman, 2017).

Therefore, with the reach and scope of impact for HR professionals growing steadily it is now more important than ever to deliver on core business responsibilities in addition to building capabilities in new and emerging areas of growth. It is important that we maintain energy and momentum in order to facilitate the required change and drive progression. The HR professionals who can confidently step up and take accountability and who set themselves challenging goals linked to their business strategy are proven to achieve the best results and enjoy higher levels of personal success. They deliver more £s per hour in value for themselves and their employers, and they often enjoy the success of being part of high-performing teams in dynamic organizations.

In Chapter 1 we looked at defining three goals that you want to work on as part of your development activity. Now to expand on that, next to each goal write what percentage of energy and effort you are putting into achieving that goal. If you have written 100 per cent, how is it that you haven't achieved these things already? Make a note if you need to so you can work on this later.

Where you have any percentage that is less than 100, ask yourself why that would be and consider what it is that might be stopping you from giving 100 per cent right now. Make a note of those things and separate the list into personal and professional.

In a work context, think about your role and the last day you were at work. What percentage of effort and energy did you put into your work? Then think about the next day you are due to work; what percentage will you give in your current role right now? If it's less than 100 for either scenario, ask yourself why that might be and make a note of anything that comes to mind. Typical explanations could be:

- You are new to the role or company and are still learning, so not 100 per cent up to speed just yet.
- You are bored and no longer challenged by your role or engaged with it.
- There might be some technological or system issue that is holding back your progress and ability to achieve.
- Perhaps your mind is just elsewhere, with lots going on at home or some level of interpersonal conflict with a colleague.
- Perhaps you're feeling a little under the weather right now, maybe you have a cold or are just feeling run down and tired.
- Is the working environment right for you? Is your workspace set up in the right way for you to succeed?

- Perhaps someone else is making the decisions regarding your work right now. Are you empowered to make the progress you want to?

Be honest with yourself and find the answer for the missing percentages; find the block that's holding you back and write it down. In calling it out and clearly identifying it you can then take positive steps to address it.

Why is this important?

If you think about your percentage contribution in terms of money, the 100 per cent effect becomes quite clear. For example, if you earn £60,000 and you are operating from a position of excellence, with 100 per cent energy and effort directed to achieving your goals, 100 per cent of your time is worth £60,000. But if something is holding you back and you happen to be operating from a position of 80 per cent, you could be losing 20 per cent of your true potential, equating to a financial value of £12,000 over a year. For someone earning a salary of £100,000 this figure increases to £20,000!

This also works for the self-employed too. What's the value of your time, and what is your earning target for this year? When you have your earning target you have your 100 per cent capacity value.

If you have ever led a team of people you can imagine how this would roll up if you expand this principle to five, ten or maybe more individuals. Imagine the value of getting just 1 per cent more energy and effort from everyone in a 10-person team where everyone made £40,000 per year. Well, 1 per cent of £40,000 is £400 and if you could multiply that by 10 people that would give you an increased ROI energy and commitment value of £4,000 over the year. If everyone in the team could up their game by 10 per cent you would have an added value level of £40,000 for the year! The equivalent of an additional head!

The bottom line is, it makes commercial sense to identify and remove blockers that impact on drive and passion. People who can effectively deliver and add value in their roles go on to be more successful, and their personal wealth increases as they gain the recognition for this. They become great role models and leaders and often go on to inspire other people to put in the effort and achieve great things too! Businesses which recognize this achieve a greater ROI for their payroll spend and gain a reputation for growing, maintaining and inspiring talent. They become the place where everyone wants to work. High-performing people create high-performing teams and those extra percentage contributions all go on to create a high-performance culture where people are empowered, engaged and inspired to achieve.

Bouncebackability

Bouncebackability is one of the most important skills you can have in your HR toolkit for the single reason that you're going to need to use it often, particularly if you're passionate about what you do and driven to make a real impact in your career. This comes down to your ability to take a risk, get a knock-back, then refocus and reposition quickly in a professional way. It's not easy but it is possible. When I first approached Ben Lewis, CEO of River Island with the idea to create Style Studio, a commercial venture outside of my HR remit, you can be sure he didn't agree to it the first time I mentioned it to him. The idea got knocked back again and again, and each time I had to reassess and learn from it. I invested more of my personal time outside of work in research and invested more time in ensuring we had a *great* HR function to allay any concerns that there was still an important job that needed to be done there too. I channelled every ounce of bouncebackability that I could find, continued to reframe my proposition, and eventually after about six months the proposal was signed off and the work began to turn the Style Studio vision into reality.

Conclusion

It's important to take some time out to think about what drives you, decide on what's important to you, and what sets your soul on fire. Sure, you're not essentially going to find that in every job you take but knowing this reduces your chances of a career misstep and helps you understand what's going on if you find things aren't going too well. Passion and drive are going to get you through the tough times and enable you to bounce back quickly and positively when you need to. Tapping into your true passion and channelling it into the work you do is probably the single most important element of commercial success. It's where you find your authentic and best self and people are going to *love* that.

Toolkit essentials: 5 steps to effectively channelling your drive and passion

1 Identify your true passion and use it to help define your personal USP.

2 Ensure that your existing goals are aligned with your true and authentic passion.

3 Create a movement and ambassadors who will support you.

4 Identify any blockers that are impacting on your motivation and drive.

5 Develop and deploy bouncebackability.

Questions for reflection

Q. What's your passion and how are you leveraging it to deliver competitive advantage for yourself and where relevant the organization that employs you?

Q. Do you have the capacity and desire to achieve just 1 per cent more in your career?

Q. What's blocking you at the moment and preventing you from achieving the things you want to achieve?

References

Baldoni, J (2016) Driving passion to fulfil your purpose, *Forbes*, 29 June, available from: www.forbes.com/sites/johnbaldoni/2016/06/29/driving-passion-to-fulfill-your-purpose [accessed 19 February 2018]

Entrepreneur Magazine (nd) Unique Selling Proposition (USP), available from: www.entrepreneur.com/encyclopedia/unique-selling-proposition-usp [accessed 20 February 2018]

Lombardo, M and Eichinger, R (2009) *FYI, For Your Improvement: A guide for development and coaching*, Lominger International: A Korn/Ferry Company

Mazor, A, Sobey, A and Kunkleman, K (2017) A true HR strategy is about more than HR, *HR Times – The HR Blog*, available at: https://hrtimesblog.com/2017/11/15/a-true-hr-strategy-is-about-more-than-hr/ [ccessed 31 May 2018]

Pink, D (2009) *Drive: The surprising truth about what motivates us*, Riverhead Books, New York

Interpersonal skills 03

Introduction

Interpersonal relationships have the potential to make or break your career and I want you to think about cultivating, building and navigating them as a skill that you need to work on just like any other skill. Of course, they come in many different forms, ranging from the relationship you need to build with your boss, to networking inside and outside of your business, relationships with peers and of course the relationships you build with the people who work for you as you advance your career.

There are multiple schools of thought on the key elements that comprise interpersonal skills and one that I feel particularly resonates for HR professionals is from Lombardo and Eichinger (2009) where they observe five components to great interpersonal skills:

- relates well to all kinds of people – up, down and sideways, inside and outside the organization;
- builds appropriate rapport;
- builds constructive and effective relationships;
- uses diplomacy and tact;
- can defuse even high-tension situations comfortably.

In this chapter we will look to expand on some of the above and also introduce the importance of Emotional Intelligence (EQ) as an essential tool for your toolkit.

How will this chapter shape my thinking?

- It will help you reconnect with the value of authentic and meaningful communication both with the people you feel comfortable around and those you don't.

- It will help to shape your thinking on the importance of the smart use of emotional intelligence both for yourself and the people you work with.

- It will help you consider your existing mechanism for resolving interpersonal tension and adopt a proactive approach to skills development in this area.

Authentic and meaningful communication

In my very first HR job I was lucky enough to work with an amazing mentor who insisted I invested time every single day in getting out from behind my desk and walking around the building we were based in. It's a habit that's never left me. Don't underestimate the value of the connections you make while wandering around. People will appreciate seeing you and it opens you up to the possibility of more conversations and more authentic and natural interactions with people. Even with the multitude of digital communication methods available I still believe that human resources is not a job that you can do sitting behind a desk.

To be authentic and meaningful in your interaction with other people you need to start with being true to yourself. Avoid trying to be someone you're not or faking interest in something someone is talking to you about; it might get you through for a little while but sooner or later you're going to get found out. If someone is talking to you about something that's important to them but you're just not connecting, try asking some more questions to help your understanding of it.

If you connect with your USP as detailed in the previous chapter and remain true to this, you should find that even the most daunting interactions become a little easier.

Emotional Intelligence (EQ)

Emotional intelligence, also known as emotional quotient (EQ) seems to be one of the latest buzzwords in HR but the reality is this concept has been around for a long time. It is widely regarded that Peter Salovey and John D Mayer were the first to use this term in 1990, where they refer to a framework for emotional intelligence. They define it as: 'A form of social intelligence that involves the ability to monitor one's own and others' feelings and emotions, to discriminate among them, and to use this information to guide one's thinking and action' (Salovey and Mayer, 1990).

During my time as HR Director at River Island we effectively integrated EQ into our L&D activity for the business through various programmes led by Nebel Crowhurst, Head of Talent Development. In this section I'm delighted to share Nebel's thoughts on this subject.

Today more than ever there is increasingly compelling evidence demonstrating the link between high EQ and successful business leaders. For many years there has been an assumption that high IQ gives the edge to success yet the notion of EQ has now taken hold with the acknowledgement that effective personal and social competence has greater impact than IQ alone.

Some of us are naturally more emotionally intelligent than others; however, the good news is we can develop and grow our EQ. In my experience, for someone to develop their EQ the starting point is to build self-awareness; knowing that our responses and reactions to situations have a direct impact on those around us and being aware of this.

To me, the greatest benefit of increasing EQ is the ability to foster truly emotionally connected relationships with people. This creates a platform for greater team and business success. Leaders that attempt to drive visionary business strategies without an emotional connection to the people they are leading tend to fail, whereas those that understand the emotions of their people as well as having strong relationships will tend to instinctively know how to connect into individual emotional drivers and as such achieve greater success through people.

High EQ can assist not only with team dynamics but equally at an individual level where diplomacy is needed to manage challenging situations. What's needed is the aptitude to build rapport intuitively through the ability to exercise empathy and effective interpersonal relationships. Commonly fostering strength in empathy tends to be a challenging area and as such support with development is often required.

In practice, HR and L&D can work with individuals to heighten their self-awareness through the use of psychometric assessment tools, the results of which can be hugely beneficial to business performance. My personal experience of success with this comes from using two psychometric assessments in parallel to one another, giving a deeper level of insight. The use of EQ-i 2.0, which assesses levels of emotional intelligence, alongside Predicative Index, which provides an accurate illustration of an individual's core drivers and therefore insight into their needs, behaviours and motivators, has proven to have a powerful impact on the leadership capabilities of the senior leadership team within River Island. Not only has the focus on developing EQ increased leadership capabilities, it has shifted the mindset of how we invest in people development across all areas of the organization in turn, resulting a culture of learning and continuous development.

As with all good things there is of course a word of caution: to accurately interpret the insights that can be gathered from psychometric assessments it is vital that organizations invest in developing the skills of HR and L&D to be qualified analysts. It can have a detrimental impact to misinterpret the information contained within these complex reports and can in fact do more harm than good when handled insensitively.

In summary, placing EQ at the heart of any people development strategy is in no doubt a vital element to successfully growing and identifying organizational talent in a sustainable and effective way.

Nebel Crowhurst, Head of Talent Development, River Island.

Resolving tension

Having worked in HR for as long as I have I'm fairly confident in saying that the single biggest cause of employee relations issues is breakdown in interpersonal relationships. It's impossible to get on well with all people all of the time; even the relationships we have with those closest to us go through their ups and downs. So, when we think about how we conduct ourselves in our interactions and how we enhance our own interpersonal skills the most important thing to work on is the thing we have the most control over, *ourselves*! The truth is that we have very little if any control over how other people choose to interact with us but we can (with practice) choose how we respond and the impact we allow other people to have on us.

Something to think about when you encounter tension in interpersonal relationships is that on a basic and fundamental level, the person you are looking to interact with needs to feel heard and valued. You don't necessarily need to agree with their point of view or their personal approach to appreciate this because on one level we all share those basic needs. We all need to feel valued and to know that our voice is heard, so you have at least two things in common as a starting point. This is the key to resolving most, if not all conflicts and the secret to ensuring you can connect with the other person on this level is to maintain consistency and channel your personality during your interactions in an engaging and authentic way. The activity below will help you to practise this skill.

Activity 3: Interpersonal skills

Think of someone in the business you work in who you feel you have a great relationship with. Make a point to go and see them today and just check in with them to see if they're ok or if they fancy getting a coffee with you. I want you to be really mindful about what's going on with yourself from the moment you decide to walk towards the other person. What's your body language like, what are you thinking about, if you were to stand in front of a mirror what expression is on your face? Do you feel tension anywhere in your body? Then as you start to speak, be conscious of the tone of your voice, intonation, pace, eye contact. Just note to yourself how you feel and what's going on.

Then, straight after that, I want you to go and see someone where you feel the relationship is a bit strained at the moment and follow the same steps, noticing any differences that might come up for you. Once you are aware of any differences you can think about the reasons behind them and ask yourself, is that person mirroring back to you subconscious signals of tension that you are directing at them?

With practice and with the knowledge that the only person in control of your actions is you (not them) try stepping into the authentic persona you use when approaching someone you like and approach the other person in exactly the same way. Consider whether the response is different and if the interaction improves when you radiate positivity as opposed to tension.

I was given a key piece of advice very early on in my working life when I was working as a horse-riding instructor; I have successfully been able to utilize it in all areas of my life since then and it's particularly useful to think about in the context of interpersonal skills. The advice was, 'Treat every class as if it was your first'.

Why is this important? If you think of this in the context of teaching classes where people are learning to ride horses the stakes can be pretty high, as horses in particular are large animals with minds of their own and are particularly tuned into the emotions and verbal and non-verbal signals that happen around them. They can easily reflect and respond to the emotions of the humans who interact with them. As a horse-riding instructor, in order to get the best from the horse and from the person you are teaching you need to convey the emotion and sentiment that you want to get back, eg active engagement, concentration, care, positive energy. So in the context of business and work I encourage you to do the same. In your personal interactions, ensure you are conveying the emotion and sentiment you want to get back as your verbal and non-verbal actions will be mirrored back to you.

The other thing that I experienced as a riding instructor was very long, busy and tiring days, often starting early 6.30/7.00 am and working through into the evening. At weekends in particular it would be common for classes to start at 9.00 am and then run back to back until 6.00 pm, sometimes later. As you will appreciate, my energy level at the start of the day was somewhat higher than it was at the end. However, that's when I really needed the advice I'd been given to kick in and it really worked. I thought about how I interacted with the customers in that very first session of the day, when I was at my best, and mirrored that through to the last session. This was so important because for the customer, the session they attended *was* the first session of the day for them; they had the excitement to reflect that, had paid the same fee for the tuition and therefore deserved the best of me, equally as my first clients did. I hold true to this sentiment even now and think of it in the context of meetings and interactions. Treat every one as if it was your first because when you do that, people feel like you're engaged, they feel heard and they feel valued. Try it, you'll be amazed at the difference it makes.

Conclusion

Interpersonal skills are arguably the most important skills to hone as HR professionals. However, at times it can be easy to lose focus and place ownership for breakdowns in professional relationships entirely in the hands of another person. In doing this, ownership for resolving the issue is also passed, resulting in continued frustrations. Therefore, the key to improving skills and results in this area is first to understand yourself and take accountability for how you show up at meetings and with 1:1 connections. Then, use what you have learned to help others develop the same awareness in themselves, potentially through utilizing an emotional intelligence framework. In addition, investment in improving interpersonal skills across an entire organization has multiple benefits including enhanced customer service leading to more sales and more loyal customers, improved productivity through enhanced working practices resulting from employees communicating more effectively, and an associated reduction in tension and conflict that significantly hampers productivity and effectiveness over time.

Toolkit essentials: 5 steps to improving interpersonal relationships

1 Ensure you make time every day to walk around your working environment and connect with the people who work there.

2 Treat people with respect and in a way that you would like them to treat you (even if they're not doing so at the moment).

3 Be true to yourself; connect with and channel your USP in your interactions.

4 Project the same verbal and non-verbal cues with people you find difficult as those you use with people you don't. Consider it as a mirror of what will be reflected back to you.

5 Treat every meeting/interaction as if it was your first.

References

Lombardo, M and Eichinger R (2009) *FYI, For Your Improvement: A guide for development and coaching,* Lominger International: A Korn/ Ferry Company

Salovey, P and Mayer, J D (1990) *Emotional Intelligence,* SAGE Publishing, available from http://journals.sagepub.com/doi/abs/10.2190/DUGG-P24E-52WK-6CDG [accessed 05 February 2018]

Bravery 04

Introduction

Writing for *Inc.* magazine in 2016, Jeff Haden commented that 'Even the bravest people are afraid; they've simply found something that matters more to them than fear' (Haden, 2016). Fear is an emotion that is a natural part of being human; the flight or fight response is ingrained in us for a very good reason. In this chapter we're going to look at how we can channel our bravery to overcome unfounded fears and step outside of our comfort zone in order to advance our careers.

> **How will this chapter shape my thinking?**
>
> - It will challenge you to think about 'grit' and how you can use this to improve results.
> - It will encourage you to question your thoughts about your comfort zone.
> - It will help you understand why you feel like jumping off the learning curve when things get tough and why it's worthwhile to keep going.

Grit

If we keep doing the same things we will keep getting the same results – that's a fact! It's only by doing things differently that we will transform and reach our true potential. It's ok to be different, to be bold. But it takes a certain amount of grit to enable bravery and help us push through tough times.

Quite often we feel this most when we find ourselves on a steep learning curve and most certainly outside of our comfort zone. John Lee and Vincent Wong refer to this in their 2015 book *The Wealth Dragon Way*, explicitly stating that what normally happens when people find themselves on a learning curve and things start to get tough is that the individual most likely jumps off and jumps onto another learning curve before repeating the cycle over and over again. You can see here how applying grit and determination would enable the individual to persist with the original curve and make the breakthrough they need in order to guarantee success. Lee and Wong state, 'If you want to succeed, you can't be fickle. You have to stick to one learning curve and keep going, accepting that obstacles and pitfalls are essential parts of the learning curve. Experience is what we get when we don't get what we want.'

On the subject of grit, perhaps the most well-known text is the *New York Times* bestseller *Grit* by Angela Duckworth (2017). In this book, Duckworth examines why some people succeed and others fail, linking it back to a blend of passion and persistence she refers to as grit. One of her quotes that particularly resonates with me is this one: 'I won't just have a job; I'll have a calling. I'll challenge myself every day. When I get knocked down, I'll get back up. I may not be the smartest person in the room, but I'll strive to be the grittiest.'

I think this is important for all HR professionals, particularly if like me you hope to broaden your remit beyond your traditional function. As previously mentioned in Chapter 2, in 2015 whilst working at River Island I'm pleased to say that I founded a commercial personal styling venture called Style Studio within the business, in addition to maintaining my role as HR Director (more on this later). To many people watching from the outside this appeared to be a pretty immediate success; however, behind the scenes I can assure you that I had needed to draw on significant reserves of bravery and grit to get things to that point. There were many knockbacks along the way but it was all worth it in the end. The advice I'd give to anyone considering something similar is to pick a venture or a dream that you're prepared to fight for because you believe in it so much. That way, it's easier to be brave, to take the knockbacks, to get back up and carry on again.

How to be more brave

At times being brave is hard and it's difficult, it's by no means the easy option. So how do you push through when you're really struggling? Caspar Craven, entrepreneur, adventurer and author of *Where the Magic Happens: How a young family changed their lives and sailed around the world* (2018) has the following advice:

> The single most important ingredient I believe to being more brave is your environment and influences. The things that you allow into your world. The people you spend time with, what you read, what you watch, what you scroll through. Managing and being conscious of what is around you can be the fastest way to be more brave.
>
> Be around people and influences that lift you up, support and encourage you. As opposed to influences that find fault, criticise and pull you down.
>
> Couple that with getting really clear on what you want your future to look like, to spend time imagining it and making it so clear and compelling that it gives you reasons to be brave and step forward and embrace your future.
>
> There's a lot more (which we cover at www.thebraveyou.com) where we help people to thrive and be more brave embracing the life that they want specifically and by design.

Caspar has sailed twice around the world; once in the world's toughest yacht race and once with his wife and three young children, aged just nine, seven and two. He has built multiple successful businesses and sold one for a seven-figure sum whilst sailing the Pacific Ocean. Caspar now combines his experiences from both business and sailing the world's oceans in his current business to deliver a 'wow' experience that leaves audiences inspired and with practical, actionable takeaways for everyday use.

Caspar also comments:

> I believe that the quality of our lives is directly proportional to the amount of uncertainty we can comfortably handle. If we all lived our lives in complete certainty it would be as boring as hell. If we all lived in complete uncertainty, it would be chaotic and probably terrifying.

The trick is to get the balance right. Hence the amount of uncertainty we can comfortably handle.

It takes bravery and courage to step outside our safe and certain comfort zone. As the cliché says, though, that is where the magic happens. It's where you embrace uncertainty. Where you are brave and step forwards. I believe in what I call The Brave You. We all have a brave part inside us. A part of us that can be trained to be more brave. What I call Brave Fitness. If you make the decision to create more growth in whatever area of your life, then you'll almost certainly need to be more brave and embrace that change. There are certain truths in life around being more brave and I believe that we can all become more brave – to become more comfortable with uncertainty.

Conclusion

There are a million clichés and sayings about bravery and comfort zones; we hear them all the time. In fact, as HR professionals we probably repeat them to others on a fairly regular basis. None of this makes stepping out of your comfort zone any less scary. It is, however, an essential thing to do if you really want to grow and build your career. It's an essential trait for most businesses too, as without bravery it's unlikely that the leaders of the business will take the calculated risks required in order for the business to thrive and grow. It's also possible to consider bravery as the foundation of creativity and innovation, as without it both of these essential components of business would be severely limited.

So let's look at it like this. Your comfort zone is a nice calm place, it feels safe, it's a place where you know what happens, when it happens and why it happens. You can curl up with a nice book there and maybe a cat will come and sit on your lap if you're into that kind of thing. If anyone comes into your comfort zone they come in because you know them, you've invited them in, you know when they're leaving and it's all on your terms. Your comfort zone is the clothes you wear when you don't need to leave the house and the meal you're going to eat that you love most in all the world. It's a *really* nice place.

Because of that, it's not surprising that you want to go there often, maybe for a holiday and stay a while to chill out and relax. However, what you *can't* do is move there and set up house.

It takes grit and guts to put yourself out there, to take the knocks and get back up. To reinvent yourself and to achieve more. For you to succeed you need to seriously evaluate the impact that your environment and the company you are keeping are having on you; let go of influencing factors that no longer support you. We all have our reasons for doing what we do, we're motivated by different factors, and we all have the ability to be brave. So be brave enough to fail, brave enough to put your neck on the line when you need to.

Toolkit essentials: 5 steps to improving bravery

1 Stay on the learning curve when the going gets tough and you feel like jumping off.

2 Build grit through ensuring you are staying true to your passion; link back to your USP.

3 Work on developing an idea that sets your soul on fire, something that you believe in so strongly that you're prepared to fight for it.

4 Remember that you can't fail because even if things don't work out exactly as you had planned, you'll still have learned a lot at the end of it. You will have acquired 'experience' that you wouldn't have had before.

5 Assess your current environment and influences to ensure they are supportive of you and make the changes you need to enable you to step up and be brave.

References

Craven, C (2018) *Where the Magic Happens: How a young family changed their lives and sailed around the world*, Adlard Coles

Duckworth, A (2017) *Grit: Why passion and resilience are the secrets to success*, Penguin, London

Haden, J (2016) Be bold, be daring, be heroic: 11 habits of genuinely brave people, *Inc.com* [online] available at: https://www.inc.com/jeff-haden/11-habits-of-genuinely-brave-people-first-90-days.html [accessed 12 June 2018]

Lee, J and Wong, V (2015) *The Wealth Dragon Way: The why, the when & the how to become infinitely wealthy*, Wiley

Your personal network

Introduction

I'll be honest, for a time in my career I operated as an extremely focused, determined and relentless lone wolf when it came to my own career development. It was a strategy that served me well up to a point. However, things really started moving when I discovered the life-changing benefits of building an active personal network. I can safely say that I would not have achieved the things I have achieved without the connections and relationships I have made through networking. Being part of a great network is like being a member of a supportive community where everyone has shared interests and is ready to step in and help other people out. Therefore, as far as I'm concerned, if you're thinking about improving your personal network, the starting point should be to consider what you can give and what you can do to add value to that community.

How will this chapter shape my thinking?

- It will encourage you to consider your motivation when it comes to networking and reassess your balance of contribution.
- It will encourage you to challenge the positioning of existing networks and their influence.
- It will encourage you to think about how you might measure the return on investment both for yourself and for others with regard to networking activity.

This chapter has been contributed by Siân Harrington, Co-Founder and Editorial Director of The People Space (www.thepeoplespace. com). I am grateful to Siân for her expert insights.

Remember that scene in Netflix's hugely successful series *The Crown*, where the viewer is introduced to the Thursday Club in London's Soho? Prince Philip is seen having a raucous time with close acquaintances including Lord Mountbatten, photographer Cecil Beaton and actor David Niven while being served by young ladies sporting names such as Flo and LouLou.

Or perhaps you recall the 2014 play *Posh* and its film version *The Riot Club*, inspired by the infamous Bullingdon Club at Oxford University, with its scenes of restaurants being trashed and public-school boys swinging from chandeliers.

What these male-only secret drinking societies have in common, aside from a penchant for wild parties, immature acts and an apparent lack of respect for women, is that they are the breeding grounds for many of the establishment influencers of yesterday and today. From former UK Prime Ministers and royalty to leading newspaper barons, lawyers and City bankers, members of these clubs make up a powerful elite and epitomize what has become known as the 'old boys' network.

The dictionary defines the old boys' network as the way in which men who have been to the same expensive school or university help each other to find good jobs. In popular parlance, it has become used in reference to the preservation of social elites in general and is a term used in a number of countries in the world. In the UK, for example, Harrow and Eton have 26 Prime Ministers among their 'old boys'.

Last year an analysis by the London School of Economics of 120 years of data from the British catalogue of the elite *Who's Who* found that alumni of nine of the country's top public schools are 94 times more likely to be in the UK's elite (Reeves et al, 2017). No wonder the phrase 'It's not what you know but who you know' has become associated with this type of network.

There have been numerous political and workplace attempts to break down the old boys' network over the years. And while it is clear it still underpins many institutions, including business, there has been some movement forward. According to a 2015 report by Korn Ferry Institute on the state of European boardrooms, for example: '... the age of Europe's boardrooms as an old boys' network is over. Recruiting directors among friends and business acquaintances is heavily criticized and the few boards that still do so stand out.'

I mention this because today, we in human resources play a key role in breaking down the old boys' network in our workplaces. Nepotism has no place in the modern organization. The idea that decisions are made behind closed doors by an informal but elite group of generally white males of a certain age is anathema at a time when there is increasing evidence that more diverse leadership leads to improved business outcomes. According to Deloitte, diversity of thinking is the new frontier in business – and to get this diversity one needs to enable a wide variety of people to voice their thoughts in a safe environment, regardless of gender, ethnicity, age, disability, seniority or sexual preference (Bourke and Dillon, 2018). A truly diverse and inclusive organization that facilitates diversity of thinking enhances innovation by some 20 per cent and enables groups to spot risks, reducing these by up to 30 per cent, says Deloitte. The opposite, an organization led at the top by the old boys' network with the same 'group think' and lacking in diversity, is clearly not good for business in today's fast-changing, agile business world where innovation and risk-taking are vital for survival.

And yet, at the same time, we are vocal in our support of the benefits of other networks. From women's leadership and LGBT networks to alumni groups, the network – and its active counterpart networking – is having a renaissance in the business world. But if networks have been discredited as a way for 'elites' to get ahead, whether they deserve it or not, why is this the case?

The answer, as motivational speaker Michele Jennae says, is that networking is not just about connecting people. It's about connecting people with people, people with ideas and people with opportunities. And in today's digital age, with its ever-quickening pace of change, this is a skill we all need. And, thanks to the growth of digital collaboration services and tools, the modern face of networking is, on the whole, more inclusive, accessible and user-friendly. You don't need to go to the right school or university, or to have the right MBA or background. All you need is a digital device (be it a personal computer or mobile phone), a username and password and you can connect to people all over the world.

For today we live in a networked society, a world that is more collaborative in nature. Witness the exponential growth in social networking sites such as Facebook. According to market and consumer data provider Statista (2018) Facebook had 2.2 billion monthly active users as of January 2018 and is the most popular social network globally. Video-sharing platform YouTube is the second most popular social network, with 1.5 billion active users, while WhatsApp also comes in with over a billion active users. Digital technologies enable organizations to operate in a very different way. Instead of the traditional, hierarchical firm, with its vertically integrated, multi-divisional, top-down structure, we now have the networked organization, one based on networks of connections and linkages, both within and between companies, all tied together in co-operative relationships. These relationships allow firms to develop joint solutions to common problems, to combine resources to gain economies of scale and to enter new markets. Such relationships facilitate collaboration in areas such as marketing, production, financing and innovation.

New technologies mean employees need not all be in one location, in a physical building or even work for one firm. More and more people are 'gigging' – enjoying the flexibility of being self-employed while producing project-based work for clients they meet through any number of freelance or gig platforms, from Upwork and PeoplePerHour to legal site UpCounsel and Ikea-owned TaskRabbit. This is expedited by the 'always on' culture, thanks to the ubiquitous mobile phone and blurring of the lines between work and social time.

The so-called 'disruptor' companies – agile, entrepreneurial, constantly changing and evolving – are masters of the network. Just look at Netflix or Amazon. Both regularly transform themselves to take advantage of new market opportunities. Or Airbnb, Uber and a myriad of platform-based companies. For them, the network is the source of competitive advantage, enabling them to scale quickly and cost-effectively (though the legal situation in relation to workers as self-employed or not is increasingly being challenged, as the UK cases of Uber, City Sprint and Pimlico Plumbers illustrate).

Talking to HR Exchange Network (Stevenson, 2017) Jaclyn Lee, Senior Director HR and Head of HR Technology and Analytics at Singapore University of Technology and Design puts it succinctly:

> The future of work is becoming more agile and responsive, with purpose-built networks and new employment relationships evolving. Digital disruptions and social networking are altering how organizations hire, manage and support people, and technologies are changing the way companies operate.

In other words, the traditional norms of location- and time-based employment are diminishing, and the number of flexible and collaborative workers is growing. In such a world, businesses take the role of 'network orchestrators' and the network is inextricably tied with value creation.

Nalin Miglani, Chief Human Resources Officer and EVP of New York-based leader in analytics and operations management EXL explains it this way:

> Businesses create much greater value if they can visualize and create a network of partners that help them get 'work' done for their business in the smartest, most effective way. Smart businesses are now at the centre of an ecosystem of expert organizations that they create. Smart businesses do not try to do all the work themselves nor employ all the people that are needed to do this work (Miglani, 2017).

Management consultancy McKinsey agrees, saying that networks are defining the way work actually gets done in today's increasingly collaborative, knowledge-intensive companies. 'In our experience, companies that invest time and energy to understand their networks and collaborative relationships greatly improve their chances of making successful organizational changes', they say (Cross, Parise and Weiss, 2007).

In a world where constant adaptability, collaboration and innovation are key to survival and where the enterprise is a 'network orchestrator', the value of people is in our ability to build relationships. As Jon Ingham, author of *The Social Organization* (2017) points out, technologies such as artificial intelligence have the ability to 'do knowledge' much better than humans. The real requirement in business today, he says, is to build the best connections, relationships and conversations. And in today's fast-paced world, there is more need than ever to develop the skills to enable you to build these connections and relationships and to have these conversations quickly.

Yet, despite being social animals, many of us humans go cold at the idea of striking up a conversation with people we don't know, let alone building a relationship. Take the business networking evening. We've all been there, downing a glass of champagne and admiring the room's décor in a bid not to look uncomfortable and hoping someone interesting will make the first move and come over to us. That's as long as they are not going to bore us with a 20-minute-long sales spiel. Or worse still, decide we are not that interesting after all, eyes darting around the room as they seek their escape, thrusting a business card into our hands as they leave for someone more important. We're not alone. Research conducted by Insead (Ibarra and Hunter, 2007) following a cohort of 30 managers making their way through leadership transition over the course of two years, found that networking was one of the most self-evident and yet most dreaded developmental challenges aspiring leaders must address. Research authors Herminia Ibarra and Mark Lee Hunter say many of the managers they studied questioned why they should spend precious time on personal networking when there wasn't even time for urgent work tasks in their busy lives. The answer, the authors reply, is that these personal contacts provide important referrals, information and, often, developmental support such as coaching and mentoring. A personal network, they say, can also be a safe space for personal development and can provide a foundation for strategic networking. Being largely external and made up of discretionary links to people with whom we have something in common, what makes a personal network powerful is its referral potential, putting us in contact in as few connections as possible with the person who has the information we require. LinkedIn is a perfect example of a digital version of this.

As a journalist, networking is a tool of my trade. Back when I started out, there was no e-mail or social media. We had to rely on the good old phone, with the odd fax thrown in for fun. Right from the beginning I knew that the best way to get to the directors to whom I needed to talk was to build relationships with their personal assistants. After a few calls, when trust had been built, I would get through on the phone to the director. Hopefully, I would later meet that person at an industry event and put a face to the name. Over time, some of these business acquaintances became more than just a source for a story, becoming trusted advisers and occasionally friends.

Yet my interest in networks was really sparked in my last corporate role, where as editor and then publishing director of an HR business magazine I was involved in launching a number of network-based activities for our readers. It was through this that I realized the power of networks is far beyond the connections you make that help you to move ahead in your career or to gain knowledge. Yes, networking has enabled me to land the scoop first. Yes, networking has enabled me to navigate the workplace politics and boardroom shenanigans of cut-throat media businesses. And yes, networking has helped me and my teams to deep dive into an industry and produce award-winning publications. However, more importantly than all the above, being involved in a safe-space network has enabled me to discover more about myself. Ultimately, the support – and challenge – I received from a handful of people in these networks gave normally risk-adverse me the strength to take a jump out of the corporate world and to become an entrepreneur.

For entrepreneurs, the business benefits of networking are well documented. From increasing sales through connections and lowering costs by working together in collaborative networks, to knowledge sharing, reputation building and the psychological benefits of sharing problems and alleviating your isolation, networking can bring real benefits.

Research conducted in 2012 by Roy M Broad, lecturer in marketing at the University of Wolverhampton, with influential business leaders in the West Midlands who were members of networks, sought to test the notion that, regardless of size, firms that have a systemized or structured approach to networking activities achieve better outcomes in terms of networking performance. It found that, generally, people do not consider how they measure the output from their networking activities. Yet, once promoted, respondents were able to distinguish what, in their opinion, equated to a return on investment in networking and to discuss how this might be measured. The most common measure was the number of referrals or sales enquiries generated through networking. The research found that networking generated an average of 25 per cent of the respondents' sales turnover and 82 per cent of respondents considered networking important to their marketing. Approximately half the respondents were members of three to five network groups.

As we have seen, research has shown personal networking helps managers transition to leadership roles. But personal networking alone is not enough, say Ibarra and Hunter. Understanding how to bring your connections to bear on organizational strategy through figuring out where to go to enlist people and groups is necessary to achieve the organizational goals:

The key to a good strategic network is leverage: the ability to marshal information, support, and resources from one sector of a network to achieve results in another. Strategic networkers use indirect influence, convincing one person in the network to get someone else, who is not in the network, to take a needed action.

Conclusion

Today there is a networking approach for everyone and every need. Digital networks enable you to plug into people all over the world that you just wouldn't reach otherwise. You can expand your reach beyond the immediate environment, usually in real time and at no or low cost. Location is no longer an issue. These networks facilitate learning, collaboration and sharing, and help you develop your personal brand, all at the touch of a button. However, there is still power in face-to-face networking. This strengthens relationships and is particularly important for business dealings. According to a report from Oxford Economics US for the US travel industry, 40 per cent of prospects become new customers after a face-to-face meeting versus just 16 per cent without, and 27 per cent of current business would be lost if it wasn't for in-person meetings (oxfordeconomics.com, 2018).

Networking is vital for career growth. It increases your profile, facilitates the exchange of information and fresh ideas, widens your support network and opens new doors. However, it can be difficult to fit into today's busy lives as it takes a significant amount of time and energy. But evidence shows it is a worthwhile investment, both for the individual and their business.

It is true that the more you put into a networking group, the more you will get out of it in terms of benefits. It is a long-term commitment and about quality, not quantity. According to Broad's research, the degree to which you are embedded in a network enhances network performance.

Networking is the number one unwritten rule of success in business, according to Sallie L Krawcheck, former president of the global wealth and investment management division of Bank of America, one of the most followed influencers on LinkedIn and one of the most senior women on Wall Street. What's important today is to think of networking in terms of collaboration and sharing, not solely about targeting business prospects, collecting cards and increasing the number of LinkedIn and Facebook contacts you have.

Successful networking is about relationship building and trust. And it's about helping others. As author and hugely popular TED presenter Simon Sinek says: 'The true value of networking doesn't come from how many people we can meet but rather how many people we can introduce to others.'

Toolkit essentials: 4 steps to improve results from networking

1 Research various network groups to find ones that are the best fit for you.

2 Actively contribute to networks that you are a member of in order to get the maximum benefit.

3 Consider how you can add value by connecting people within your network who would otherwise not have met.

4 Maintain a consistent and authentic persona both in face-to-face networking and social networks.

References

Bourke, J and Dillon, B (2018) The diversity and inclusion revolution: eight powerful truths, *Deloitte Insights*, 22, available at: https://www2.deloitte.com/insights/us/en/deloitte-review/issue-22/ diversity-and-inclusion-at-work-eight-powerful-truths.html [accessed 26 July 2018].

Broad, R (2012) Networking performance: a study of the benefits of networking in the West Midlands, available at: https://core.ac.uk/ download/pdf/17307679.pdf [accessed 02 March 2018]

Cross, R, Parise, S and Weiss, L (2007) The role of networks in organisational change, *McKinsey*, available at: *www.mckinsey.com/ business-functions/organization/our-insights/the-role-of-networks-in- organizational-change* [accessed 02 March 2018]

Ibarra, H and Hunter, M L (2017) How leaders create and use networks, *Harvard Business Review*, January, available from: *www.hbr. org/2007/01/how-leaders-create-and-use-networks* [accessed 02 March 2018]

Ingham, J (2017) *The Social Organization* Kogan Page, London

Korn Ferry Institute (2015) *Beyond The Old Boys' Network: What's happening in European boardrooms and a guide to best practices*, available at: www.kornferry.com/institute/beyond-old-boys-network- whats-happening-european-boardrooms-and-guide-best [accessed 02 March 2018]

Miglani, N (2017) Decoupling business, work and jobs: exactly where is value created in today's organisations? *The People Space*, available at: https://www.thepeoplespace.com/ideas/articles/decoupling-business- work-and-jobs-exactly-where-value-created-todays-organisations [accessed 02 March 2018]

Oxfordeconomics.com (2018) [online] The return on investment of US business travel, available at: https://www.oxfordeconomics.com/Media/ Default/Industry%20verticals/Tourism/US%20Travel%20Association- %20ROI%20on%20US%20Business%20Travel.pdf [accessed 26 July 2018]

Reeves, A et al (2017) *The Decline and Persistence of the Old Boy: Private schools and elite recruitment 1897–2016*, Sage, available at: http://journals.sagepub.com/doi/abs/10.1177/0003122417735742 [accessed 02 March 2018]

Statista (2018) Most popular social networks worldwide as of October 2018, ranked by number of active users (in millions), available at:

https://www.statista.com/statistics/272014/global-social-networks-ranked-by-number-of-users/ [accessed 02 March 2018]

Stevenson, M (2017) Disruptive tech transformations: human resources and the digital journey, *HR Exchange Network*, available at: https://www.hrexchangenetwork.com/hr-tech/reports/disruptive-tech-transformations-human-resources [accessed 07 November 2018]

Inspirational leadership 06

Introduction

According to the dictionary a leader is 'a person who rules, guides, or inspires others'. Also, leadership is defined as 'the action of leading a group of people or an organization'. The word 'inspirational' is defined as 'providing or showing creative or spiritual inspiration'. But there's more to it than that. writing for *Inc* magazine in 2017, Marissa Levin observes that 'Inspiration (not motivation) is the most important leadership trait, fuelled by passion and purpose' (Levin, 2017). Levin goes on to note that Richard Branson has also identified the ability to inspire as the single most important leadership skill and that:

According to an IBM survey of 1,700 CEOs through 64 countries, the three most important leadership traits are:

1 the ability to focus intensely on customer needs;

2 the ability to collaborate with colleagues; and

3 the ability to inspire.

(Levin, 2017)

In this chapter we look at the concept of 'Inspirational Leadership' and think about how best you can embody this as you progress through your career.

How will this chapter shape my thinking?

- It will prompt you to consider your own leadership style and impact regardless of where you currently are in your career.
- It will drive you to consider the impact of self-care on your ability to be an inspirational leader.
- It will invite you to consider how you and the business you work in demonstrate 'care' for the individuals working within the organization and the impact this has on the perception of leadership.

To be inspirational, you must first be inspired

I'm sure you will all be familiar with the difference between 'management' and 'leadership'. Management is often described as what happens when you 'tell' or instruct another person to do something and can feel like you are pushing to get the desired outcome. Leadership is what happens when people are compelled to follow and complete work or activities because they want to not because they have to. It feels more like a 'pull' motion is experienced. In this regard, I like to think of 'management' as being ruled by the head and 'leadership' as coming from the heart. It therefore becomes easier to be an inspirational and authentic leader if you are doing work you personally feel passionate about and are intrinsically connected to. You need to do work that inspires you. Your heart needs to be in it, so do work that sets your soul alight to the point that it doesn't really feel like work at all. To be inspirational, you must first be inspired.

Self-care and leadership

We all have the capability to become inspirational leaders if we choose to do so. However, in my experience a lot of people neglect an important step on this journey and that's the step of self-care. In the next chapter we will dedicate more time to this subject, specifically in relation to mental wellbeing, so for now our focus will be on self-care in relation to your ability to perform as an inspirational leader. I view it like the scenario on an aeroplane when you're instructed to put on your own oxygen mask before helping others. You need to look after yourself first to enable you to function effectively enough to really be an inspiration to other people. You need to get yourself in the right mindspace first and then you can role model this behaviour to the people you hope to lead. The great news is, though, that it's never too late to go back and take this step towards improved self-care; in fact I'd actively encourage it. Routinely plan in time to assess and review your own self-care and ensure you're still on track. It's often the case that this is the first thing we let slip when the pressure's on. The following activity will help you assess your current position with regard to your personal wellbeing.

Activity 4: Self-care assessment

Table 6.1

	Low	Average	Excellent
Physical exercise			
Mental wellbeing			
Diet			
Hobbies			
Time with friends			
Time with family			
Level of sleep			

If after doing this activity you find a number of areas sitting in the 'Low' section, consider if there's something you could do today that might move you up into the 'Average' or even 'Excellent' column.

When you are in a good position regarding your own levels of self-care you'll then be in a much healthier and authentic position to convey 'care' to the people you hope to inspire to follow you. Consider the scenario of giving this activity to your team and the people who are looking to you for inspiration, and asking them to complete it for themselves. What would you want their responses to look like? It's essential for you to role model excellent behaviours here if you want to inspire them in others. As the saying goes, 'With great power comes great responsibility', and it's true; you don't have a hope of bringing out the best in other people if you overlook this simple thing. It doesn't matter how busy you get, you still need to have the emotional intelligence to be able to consider the impact of yourself and the working environment on the team you are hoping to inspire.

Authenticity

As a leader it's important to stay true to yourself so you can be honest and authentic in what you do. People appreciate that and if you try to be something you're not they're going to see through it pretty quickly. Particularly with the prevalence of social media, if you're not being genuine people are going to pick up on it more quickly and more publicly than they would have done before. In his 2013 book *Crush It! Why now is the time to cash in on your passion*, Gary Vaynerchuk makes reference to a scenario where Patrick Doyle, CEO of Domino's pizza, effectively responded to an incident where two of his employees had filmed themselves doing something disgusting to the food and then posted it on YouTube. This could have been a potentially brand-destroying action, but Vaynerchuk praises the fact that Doyle responded in the same media, ie YouTube, and averted a crisis, stating, 'I respect how fast they got into the trenches and responded via the same medium.' However, he also notes that there could have been an even better outcome if Doyle had looked into the camera more and 'lost the script', effectively amplifying his authenticity and speaking more from the heart. This would have had the result of amplifying the perceived level of care. Vaynerchuk is himself a great example of someone who epitomizes authenticity through laying his entire life bare for his legions of 'followers' to be inspired by.

Rest, and creating space to cultivate a vision

Research from the Hult International Business School identified that lack of sleep can significantly hinder an individual's ability to perform. The blog summarizing the results observes that healthy adults should get a minimum of seven hours of sleep a night, but most people average less than that. The article highlights the fact that 'It is common for managers and colleagues to look at a lack of focus or motivation, irritability, and bad decision making as being caused by poor training, organizational politics or the work environment. The answer could be much simpler – a lack of sleep' (Reynolds, 2016).

Another important facet of inspirational leadership is acknowledging and embracing the need for rest and downtime. I've lost count of the number of CEOs I've spoken to who have had sleep issues and were unable to switch off. I don't care what anyone says about being able to survive on three hours sleep a night; we're all human and we need to sleep, and, in any event, who wants to just 'survive' or 'get by'? Surely if you're reading this your ambitions are a little bit higher. If you're having trouble sleeping, it's really important to address this. Look at your lifestyle choices and use of stimulants; how do you unwind? How calm is the environment in which you sleep? I take this seriously because as a leader, other people and the organization you work in are going to be relying on you to be the one to come up with the master plan. You need to have the overall vision that is so inspirational that it will compel other people to join you in making it happen. If you're feeling burned out and sleep deprived the chances of you coming up with the vision that's commercially viable and inspiring are pretty slim. If you don't give yourself the space to think and create the vision for your business or business unit, know that someone else will step in and do it, thereby assuming the leadership role by proxy. There are specific implications of this that we'll look at in Chapter 9 where we focus on 'People and Culture' and consider influencers and decision makers and their impact on how things really get done – sometimes even to the detriment of a leader's credibility.

Care for others

Do all leaders care about other people? Do they care about the people working in the businesses they run and in the supply chains that support them? No, sadly they don't and I'm sure you've seen stories reflecting this hitting the press from time to time. Sometimes large and successful businesses seem to get by in this way with a figurehead who seemingly puts profit over people. Are these businesses seen as successful? Yes. But at what long-term cost? You have to question how sustainable the practice is, particularly in an age when people are more concerned about the moral consequences of such behaviour. We've seen the backlash against the gig economy and customers boycotting certain businesses as a result of negative press about their employment practices or use of labour in their supply chains. The government is starting to take this more seriously and there is a swell of motion to create better workplaces and working lives for all.

Conclusion

To be an 'inspirational' leader you really are going to need to care and to show this to your team and employees in the same way a commercial business shows care to its customers. To care you have to be authentic and genuine and you need to know your people; you need to have meaningful interactions with them. Through this you become more inspirational, as people know you will be honest with them and that you've got their back. Through caring you develop a mutual sense of trust and when people trust you and are inspired by you they'll have your back too and will do what it takes to help you develop the vision and turn it into reality.

Toolkit essentials: 5 steps to inspirational leadership

1 Do work that inspires you.

2 Maintain a high level of your own personal self-care.

3 Be honest and authentic in everything you do.

4 Allow yourself time to cultivate the vision.

5 Care about others.

Questions for reflection

Q. How happy are you with your own level of personal self-care? What actions will you take to improve this?

Q. Do you see evidence of poor self-care in members of the leadership team in the business you currently work in? What are you going to do about this?

Q. In what ways can the business you work in improve the way it demonstrates 'care' to the people who work within the business. How can you initiate this?

References

Collinsictionary.com (2018) Leadership, available at: www.collinsdiction-ary.com/dictionary/english/leader [accessed 12 June 2018]

Levin, M (2017) Why great leaders (Like Richard Branson) inspire instead of motivate, *Inc.*, available at: www.inc.com/marissa-levin/why-great-leaders-like-richard-branson-inspire-instead-of-motivate.html [accessed 12 June 2018]

Oxforddictionaries.com (2018a) Leadership, available at: https://en.oxforddictionaries.com/definition/leadership [accessed 12 June 2018]

Oxforddictionaries.com (2018b) Inspirational, available at: https://en.oxforddictionaries.com/definition/inspirational [accessed 12 June 2018]

Reynolds, K (2016) How sleep deprivation affects work and performance? [Infographic], *Hult Blog*, available at: www.hult.edu/blog/how-sleep-deprivation-affects-work-and-performance/ [accessed 12 June 2018]

Vaynerchuk, G (2013) *Crush it! Why now is the time to cash in on your passion*, HarperBusiness

Self-care and mental wellbeing 07

Introduction

According to a Deloitte study in 2017, each year more than one in four people in the general population and one in six in the workforce is likely to be suffering from a mental health condition (Deloitte, 2017). The report draws attention to the fact that 'presenteeism from mental ill health alone costs the UK economy £15.1 billion per annum, in what is almost twice the business cost as actual absence from work,' and that 'The total cost of mental ill health to UK employers was estimated at £26 billion, costing £1,035 per employee, per year in 2007.' Quite staggering figures and perhaps even more so when you consider that a lot of people are still hesitant about disclosing mental health issues and therefore they can go unreported.

It may be something that isn't talked about as much as it should be, but the fact is that it is imperative for us to focus on mental health and wellbeing, both of other people and of ourselves. While every individual needs to play their part in assessing and improving their emotional and mental health, this holds especially true for HR professionals, leaders and those in senior positions who are responsible to some degree or other for taking care of the health and wellbeing of the people who work for them. In this chapter we turn our focus to mental wellbeing and explore the implications of this for the organizations we work in and also for ourselves as human resources practitioners.

How will this chapter shape my thinking?

- It will encourage you to improve your own mental wellbeing and identify ways to protect it.

- It will enable you to identify basic symptoms of concern in others and suggest immediate actions you can take to assist them.

- It will provide you with a wider context and information to support you in setting up programmes to support the organizations you work for.

Context

The World Health Report by the World Health Organization doesn't make for happy reading, with data suggesting that mental health illnesses or disorders will affect about one in four people at any point in their lives – and the numbers are only increasing, that too at an alarming rate (World Health Organization, 2013). A report published by the Mental Health Foundation in 2016 detailed that nearly half of all adults think that they have had a diagnosable mental health issue at some point in their life (Mental Health Foundation, 2016). The positive here, however, is that in the main, people no longer shy away from talking about mental health and wellbeing or consider the subject a taboo like they did not too long ago. People have generally become more accepting of such subjects regardless of whether or not they strike certain chords and evoke emotions that most would much rather not deal with – and even though it's a slow start, it's a good start. As an HR practitioner, it's important for you to play your part in diminishing the stigma attached to mental health issues and also to equip the individuals and organizations you work with to do the same. But it can be hard to know where to start and while the majority of people already know what needs to be done in order to improve their physical health, the same can't necessarily be said about mental health. In fact, since talking about mental health illnesses and disorders is only just starting to become destigmatized, most people aren't even sure what's going on inside their heads let alone able to take positive steps to improve it.

Causes and focus

It is important for all HR professionals to understand the possible causes or contributing factors that can lead to the development of mental illnesses or unhealthy mental states.

Even though the number of people who have developed mental illnesses or disorders due to childhood trauma or unfortunate events in their lives may be high, mental illnesses and disorders can also be genetic or hereditary problems that run in families for generations. Infections or injuries, too, can be responsible for mental illnesses. In addition, long-term substance abuse can be responsible for the development of mental health diseases and disorders.

According to The Health and Safety Executive (2018), there are six main areas that can lead to work-related mental health issues, specifically: the demands of the job; the level of control people have over how to do the work; the degree of support they receive to do the job; relationships with co-workers and managers; lack of understanding about their role and responsibilities; and lack of engagement through periods of change.

Since the list of possible causes and contributing factors is exhaustive, it is important for organizations to focus on creating a multifaceted solution instead of a temporary fix that may not address the problem at root level regardless of their size or the number of employees they employ. While most organizations are already working on strategies to improve the mental and emotional health of their staff, it is imperative for managers and leaders in organizations that are not already onboard with this to take the lead and be the pioneers of change in the right direction.

How does mental health affect an entire organization?

According to the World Health Organization, a healthy work environment is 'one in which there is not only an absence of harmful conditions, but an abundance of health-promoting ones' (World

Health Organization, nd). And, as mentioned above, the mental health of employees is related to their overall health and wellness. With that said, it is safe to assume that someone with better mental health will fall sick much less and for shorter durations than someone whose mental health isn't quite at its best. However, a decrease in the number of off days that your employees take is not the only reason you should be concerned about their mental health. A healthier and happier state of mind will not only help people be more focused at what they're doing, it will also help them be more productive and strive for better and improved results. Writing for *Forbes* in 2017, Camille Preston notes that according to one study, happy employees are up to 20 per cent more productive than unhappy ones, and in relation to sales the impact is even greater, with happy employees raising sales by 37 per cent (Preston, 2017). Despite the digital transformations that are underway in practically every industry under the sun, businesses, companies and organizations are beginning to realize that the human component is key and that the overall health and wellness of employees has been put on the back seat for far too long.

As important as the absence of pressurizing and stress-inducing factors may be for the growth of any business and its employees on a personal and professional level, the necessity of a work environment that is positive cannot be underestimated when it comes to the overall health of the organization. An improved and happier state of mental wellbeing within an organization can contribute directly to more competitive advantages. Any environment or workplace that cultivates positivity and shows concern for the mental, physical and psychological wellbeing of employees is one in which talent will thrive and grow and that's what the primary goal of any business, company or organization should be when it comes to the employees they are responsible for. Essentially, good mental health and wellbeing is a plus for the entire cycle, from customers to employers. Organizations that focus on the mental health and wellbeing of their employees do not only have better figures for employee retention, but since these employees are more motivated, dedicated and productive, the results of focusing on mental health and wellbeing can pretty much speak for themselves.

HR professionals are not immune

Whilst it can be a very natural thing for HR professionals to understand the importance of mental wellbeing and apply good practices in the organizations they work in, something that's not discussed enough is the subject of mental wellbeing for HR practitioners themselves.

There are very few professions with such varied and substantive demands on an individual's personal wellbeing, and where adequate training to enable an individual to meet these demands is not provided as a core part of an education curriculum. Some scenarios to consider are:

- supporting people with life-limiting or terminal illnesses (or where employees have family members with the same);
- responding to the aftermath of terrorist attacks where employees have been at the scene;
- employees being assaulted or murdered at work;
- employees accused of paedophilia;
- employees becoming involved in extremist activity;
- investigating claims of sexual harassment;
- attempted and/or actual suicide of employees;
- response to natural disasters where employees are based in that location;
- a requirement to mediate conflict between colleagues;
- management of disciplinary and grievance cases;
- management of redundancy processes;
- events in the HR professional's own personal life.

This is an important point to reflect on when you consider that all of the above and many other examples not listed here may have crossed the path of an individual working in HR.

Then, add to this the unique positioning of HR within organizations and the additional demands that this can bring. There are very few roles within an organization where individuals working within that function, from entry level up to executive, are required to contribute across the entirety of the organization, resolve problems and support every other function. It is an amazing positioning of opportunity for HR professionals but one that does not come without unique challenges not always faced by individuals working in other functions. Then layer on to that the demands and expectations that this is not just a role of support and the level of commercial contribution required is going to be high, and a delicate balancing act is needed to ensure individuals within the function can perform without risk of overwhelm.

It's not just work-related stress that can have an impact on HR professionals either; often factors outside of work can play a significant role. My own journey is an example of this, where in 2017 I personally experienced a breakdown caused by factors arising in my life outside of work. The thing that surprises a lot of people is that I didn't see it coming and it was all so sudden and unexpected. At the time I thought things were great, though looking back I can now see the triggers and signs that were impossible to pick up on at the time. For me, work had actually become a coping mechanism and a focus that enabled me to detach and distance myself from unresolved traumatic events that I really should have been dealing with. Eventually my body and mind gave me a very clear message that I needed to address this and I ultimately found myself sitting in A&E on a Saturday morning with waves of intense pain, not knowing if I was having a heart attack or a stroke. I can tell you that certainly provides a wake-up call that you can't ignore. I count myself as fortunate that in fact my physical symptoms were the result of a panic attack and not a heart attack as I had originally feared. The shock, pain and intensity of the experience still stay with me and I'm grateful for that as it's a good reminder to prioritize health and wellbeing. The experience has also enabled me to spot the symptoms of a potential breakdown in others and support them at an early stage. In addition, I now also support individuals who require help in returning to work following psychological breakdown.

So, how do you look after yourself and promote your own self-care in order to keep yourself healthy and perform at a high level?

Three easy tips to help you build your own mental strength and resilience

1 **Triggers.** Identify any current triggers for negative emotions or sources of stress in your life and write them down. Next, separate the list into the ones you can do something about and the ones you can't. With the ones you can't change, give yourself permission to let them go and release them. You can't change them but you can change the way you react to them. If you really can't change it no amount of worry or stress will influence that specific thing and the worry and stress will only affect you in a negative way. Relax your shoulders, let those things go as they are not your burdens to carry. Own what's yours to deal with and get the professional help you need to get through those issues; you do not need to do this all by yourself. With the things you *can* influence and change, just pick one thing that you can do each day that will make that situation better. Start small but start today; do just one thing to improve the situation.

2 **Hydration.** This is such a simple factor but one that can be particularly destructive if not taken care of. The fact is, if you're not properly hydrated there is no way you will be able to operate at peak performance and you will be much more prone to experiencing the impact of stress and anxiety. You're also likely to experience a degree of 'brain fog' which will slow you down further, adding to your problems. Then there's the fact that your body physically needs water to survive and to enable nutrients to be absorbed and keep you in top shape. Ensure you're drinking the right amount of water and also look at supplementing with electrolytes to enhance the benefits.

3 **Diet and exercise.** Review your current diet and exercise routine and make any changes needed to improve it. With exercise, find something that works for you and take the option to walk a few more times during the day when you might not otherwise have done so. Look to reduce your caffeine intake and also reduce the amount of refined sugar you consume too. Consider this in the context of a high-performing race horse; its trainer wouldn't feed it junk food and alcohol and then expect it to perform and yet we do this to ourselves all of the time. Again, small changes are the key here to sustaining positive change.

Improving the mental health and wellbeing of employees

HR professionals and business leaders can make a lot of difference to the overall state of emotional and mental health and wellbeing in any business, company or organization and the impact they make can be enhanced if they intervene early instead of as a response to major problems within the organization. There are some simple steps to follow to get started on this journey.

Initial assessment and review

Reviewing the current activities, processes and policies within the organization where you work is the extremely crucial first step that will help you assess how much importance is being given to mental health and wellbeing in your business. You could run anonymous surveys or polls asking questions about how your employees feel they are being treated in the workplace, and whether or not they believe that the organization is supporting their mental or emotional health. Once you get their responses, you will be able to gain a lot of insights about the general perception of the system and be able to pinpoint which processes or activities are proving to be detrimental. Once you have identified the challenges and hazardous processes within your business, you will be able to develop a more comprehensive solution to tackle the problem.

Identification of risks

The symptoms and risks associated with mental health issues and disorders are generally not as easy to spot as those for physical problems, conditions or diseases, and any help pertaining to this will not only be appreciated, but will also prove to be highly advantageous and beneficial. In fact, an initiative as apparently small and insignificant as placing posters explaining the importance of focusing on your mental health and wellbeing can go a long way and prove to your employees that you really do care. But that won't be enough to get the job done. If you're trying to deal with the issue at root level, it is important for you to help your employees figure out the state of their mental health and wellbeing whilst respecting confidentiality and privacy. Since posters will not do the trick for everyone on a personal level, you can take things up a notch and invite a team of mental health professionals to support. An example of a service fairly new to this space is Sanctus, based in London, UK, whose mission is to change the perception of mental health and put the world's first mental health gym on the high street (https://sanctus.io/). Inviting professionals to your organization in this way will not only be a more comprehensive step in the process, but will also help your employees understand that your concern in the previous stage was sincere and that you're dedicated to playing your part.

Promote a balanced lifestyle

As an HR professional and in collaboration with the leaders of your organization, you are responsible for ensuring that employees are not working too many hours as stress and the pressure of work can take a toll on their mental and physical health. Even though work and deadlines should be given importance, it is crucial for you to step up when you hear reports of employees at risk due to not focusing on their physical, mental or emotional wellbeing, and help them draw the line between personal and professional life. Here, leading by example can do a lot more than mere words. It is therefore essential that you role model good behaviours here and do not contradict the message you are providing, thereby removing credibility in any mental wellbeing programmes that have been introduced.

Mental first aid training

First aid training is already a priority for most companies and organizations, but training for mental health and related issues is something that is yet to be normalized. As an HR professional, it is imperative for you to promote mental first aid training and ensure that people know not only how to react, but also what to do in case someone in your workplace is dealing with an emotional or mental health issue.

There are now a growing number of options for provision of this, one example being the Mental Health First Aid training provided by MHFA England, who also provide a model for first contact and how to approach an individual in need of assistance.

Conclusion

Supporting and promoting the improvement of mental health is something that every HR professional, leader and manager should start focusing on more to ensure the wellbeing and performance of employees within an organization. In addition, HR professionals should pay particular attention to their own mental health and take positive steps to protect it and role model good behaviours in order to inspire others and add credibility to mental wellbeing initiatives.

Toolkit essentials: 5 steps to protect your own mental wellbeing

1 Ensure you are eating a healthy diet and exercising appropriately.

2 Manage your workload in such a way that you do not need to work excessive hours and become part of a long-hours culture.

3 Explore options for practising mindfulness or meditation.

4 Build strong personal and professional networks.

5 Do not hesitate to ask for help when you need it.

Questions for reflection

Q. How happy are you with your own level of mental wellbeing? What actions will you take to improve this?

Q. How is mental wellbeing for employees promoted in the organization you work in? Who takes the lead on this?

Q. In what ways can the business you work in improve the way it manages issues of mental health? How can you initiate this?

References

Deloitte (2017) At tipping point? Workplace mental health and wellbeing, available at: www2.deloitte.com/content/dam/Deloitte/uk/Documents/public-sector/deloitte-uk-workplace-mental-health-n-wellbeing.pdf [accessed 12 June 2018]

Health and Safety Executive (2018) Stress at work: causes, *HSE*, available at: www.hse.gov.uk/stress/causes.htm [accessed 27 Jul 2018]

Mental Health Foundation (2016) Fundamental facts about mental health 2016, available at: www.mentalhealth.org.uk/publications/fundamental-facts-about-mental-health-2016 [accessed 27 July 2018]

Preston, C (2017) Promoting employee happiness benefits everyone, *Forbes*, available at: www.forbes.com/sites/forbescoachescouncil/2017/12/13/promoting-employee-happiness-benefits-everyone/#596fa9ac581a [accessed 27 July 2018]

World Health Organization (nd) Stress at the workplace, available at: www.who.int/occupational_health/topics/stressatwp/en/ [accessed 07 November 2018]

World Health Organization (2013) World Health Report, available at: www.who.int/whr/en/ [accessed 07 November 2018]

PART TWO
Know your business

Product

08

Introduction

In this chapter we focus our attention on the 'product' your business sells in order to generate revenue. In order to be a credible influencer in your organization it's essential that you not only know about the nature of the products sold by your business; you must go beyond surface-level awareness in order to understand the 'why' and 'how' of the product in addition to the 'what'.

How will this chapter shape my thinking?

- It will give you a deeper understanding of the purpose of the business you work in.
- It will give you insights that will enable you to target your work more effectively.
- It will help you to identify new ways to add value.
- It will encourage you to consider the ethical responsibilities of your business in relation to supply chain.

What, why and how?

You probably already have a good idea of how the business you work for makes money, specifically in relation to the product or service they sell. Here we'll take a deeper dive and consider the relevance of this on your role and look at the potential impact you can make through enhancing your knowledge in this area.

What it is should be straightforward; it could be stationery, professional services, clothing etc. However, if you are in any doubt the first thing you need to do is go and find out. Take this as a priority action;

go out into your business today and get some answers. It can be an interesting activity to get some views from different parts of your organization too. For example, speak to colleagues in Marketing, Finance, Buying, Design and Sales and get their views.

As a prompt for your conversations, the first thing to consider is establishing the purpose of the product – why does it exist and who is it for? Does the business have a target customer profile? How and when does the customer use or engage with your product? Through this you start to build up a more comprehensive picture of why your business exists and the impact it is having in the world.

It is also useful to understand the key features of the product – how is the range of lines or services categorized? If you have multiple products it's essential to look at this in the context of the full range from entry to exit point. Where are the most profitable lines? Which are the least profitable and why are they still there?

Lifecycle

If it's not already documented within your business, map out the lifecycle of your product right through from design to point of sale. Consider this in relation to what people are required to support each stage, whether these are areas of skills growth or decline, and determine any potential skills gaps for the future. This gives you one tier of understanding and also a valuable insight that can be shared with new recruits as part of your onboarding process. You then also need to consider 'lifecycle' from a marketing perspective, with the four phases of this lifecycle being as follows:

1 **Introduction to the market.** This is typically where sales of this particular item are lower, costs are higher, there are fewer competitors and customers are early adopters.

2 **Growth.** In this phase of the lifecycle sales increase and costs usually fall, leading to increased profits. The customer base grows as the credibility of the product becomes more established and awareness starts to increase. Also, with increased awareness comes an increase in competition from similar brands and service providers.

3 Maturity. Here the product achieves peak sales and this is the point where profits are highest. Typically the product is now mass market and the number of competitors has levelled out. In this phase the customer demographic may shift a little and depending on the nature of the product early adopters may well have moved on to the next emerging thing.

4 Decline. In this phase sales are falling and profits are decreasing. The customer base will contract and the number of competitors will also fall.

This is important to understand from a staffing and engagement perspective, as you will find that the support you need to provide to the business unit during these phases will need to adapt in line with them. You will need to consider resourcing requirements as the work scales and contracts, as well as the skill base required. The innovation and drive required in a growth phase will not play the same role as the product hits maturity and then decline. Consider how you keep people motivated and engaged through these phases.

Costs

When you have an understanding of the product and its lifecycle you can then dig down deeper to explore costs associated with the product or product line. You will need to establish the base or 'cost' price of the product and then consider it in relation to the 'retail' price. How does your business calculate the mark-up and what is the product margin? Product margin is usually straightforward to work out as per the example below:

1 Establish the cost of producing the goods, or 'cost of goods sold', for example £20.

2 Establish the revenue (how much are the goods sold for, for example £100).

3 Calculate the gross profit by subtracting costs from revenue (£100 – £20 = £80).

4 Divide gross profit by revenue: £80 / £100 = 0.8.

5 Express it as percentages: 0.8 x 100 = 80%.

As you start to look into the costs of creating the product you will establish that there are some 'fixed' and some 'variable' costs.

Fixed costs: a fixed cost is something that will not change as the volume of product sold increases and decreases.

Variable costs: variable costs will change in relation to the volume of product sold. They typically rise as production increases and fall as production decreases.

We'll explore this a little further and cover budgeting later on in Chapters 11 and 12, so for now I want you to start to collect some data on how these costs break down for the business you work in specifically in relation to product. Then, reflect on any areas where you feel operating costs could be reduced in order to increase the margin.

Supply chain

For most businesses their success or failure can hinge on the effectiveness of their supply chain and there are a lot of considerations here for HR professionals.

It can be interesting to look at how your company views the individuals working within your supply chain as a starting point. If you reflect on the fact that supply chain effectiveness can make or break a business, it makes sense to ensure that the 'human' component of the chain is being treated in a way that enables peak performance. There is perhaps no greater example of this than the Rana Plaza tragedy of 2013, where 1,138 workers lost their lives in a clothing factory in Bangladesh. Closer to home, issues have also come to light regarding concerns over UK factories in Leicester described as a 'ticking time bomb' in a *Telegraph* news article in August 2017 (Armstrong, 2017). What role can and should HR play?

A significant step forward with regard to the above occurred in 2015, when the Modern Slavery Act came into place in the UK. This applies to all companies with a turnover, or group turnover of £36 million or more and which are incorporated in or carry out business in the UK. The Act requires companies to publish an annual statement detailing the actions they have taken to ensure that slavery and human trafficking are not taking place anywhere in their own businesses or in their supply chain. This is a perfect opportunity for HR professionals to extend their remit into this area if they are not already doing so and add value to the wider 'people' agenda for the organizations they support.

Aside from the human and reputational impact of supply chain issues there is a direct financial consequence to performance or underperformance in this business area. A great example of how this can go spectacularly wrong was when KFC overhauled its British supply chain in November 2017 and switched to a new distributor for its chicken with the intention of revolutionizing its UK food service supply chain. The outcome was somewhat different to that, with a result that in February 2018 two-thirds of its branches were closed due to delivery problems and a chicken shortage. Three key lessons in relation to this were pulled out by Kevin O'Marah for *Forbes* in March 2018. First, the 'food supply chain is different', therefore suggesting that because of the specific requirements of this industry different considerations need to be applied when considering any retendering process and agreements. Second, 'logistics should not be viewed as a cost centre' that can be cut to the wire, and finally, 'customers can be coaxed'. This was in relation to the humour and brilliant marketing the company applied in response to the issue, which went some way to winning over the hearts of their customers and even potentially attracting new ones.

It's also important to note what happens when things go well, and a brilliant example of this is the fashion retailer Zara, whose supply chain is attributed as being 'the source of its competitive advantage' (Gorepatti, 2017). Writing for *Digitalist* magazine, Gorepatti observes that the key operational theme for the retailer is agility across product development, manufacturing and supply chain. Zara's supply chain is set up in such a way that a product can go from a sketch to being in a store in less than six weeks. When you look at that in the context of the fact that they also carry upwards of 11,000 distinct items per year in comparison to the average 4,000 of competitors, the advantage of a slick and efficient supply chain becomes clear.

How can HR professionals get involved?

I spoke to Katie Jacobs, editor of *Supply Management* magazine, to get her views on challenges organizations are currently facing in relation to supply chain and also her thoughts on how HR professionals can add value in this area.

1 From your observations, what are the top three hot topics in relation to supply chain at the moment?

Supply chain strategy is becoming increasingly important to businesses for a myriad of reasons, from cutting costs to reducing risk, becoming more agile and innovative, and meeting increasingly complex consumer demands. Thus many of the issues facing supply chains and the procurement/supply function are the same as those facing business in general and other functions (including HR), such as the desire to move from being transactional to being strategic, the ability to deal with a fast pace of change, and the need to embrace a higher level of automation and digitization. But I would pick out the following three issues as hot topics for the industry.

Modern slavery: there are 40.3 million people in slavery worldwide and 16 million of them are forced into working for companies. This makes the risk of finding forced labour in the supply chain of prime importance for all organizations and sectors. This is not just a risk in far-flung places either; according to Home Office estimates there are 13,000 victims of modern slavery in the UK. High-profile cases in the UK include a chicken farm (Happy Eggs being collected by not so happy workers), a bedmaker supplying John Lewis, and traffickers recruiting and controlling vulnerable migrants to work at Sports Direct's warehouse. The 2015 Modern Slavery Act requires every business with a turnover of more than £36 million and a footprint in the UK to publish an annual transparency statement about what they are doing to tackle modern slavery. There are some brands leading the way; the Co-op's Bright Futures programme, for example, gives work experience and job opportunities to slavery victims.

Change and volatility: the pace of change will never be so slow as it is today, but it is hard enough to keep up in 2018. Global markets remain volatile, exacerbated by forces such as increased protection-ism in the United States and the impact of Brexit on currency markets and commodity prices. Supply chains need to be agile and able to respond quickly to change. This requires new models and mindsets. Some businesses are even redesigning their entire models around supply chains (eg consumer goods firms selling direct to consumers). Procurement needs need to support innovation in order to support change, which leads to...

Digitization and Industry 4.0: Blockchain, AI, the Internet of Things... connected and automated supply chains are becoming more of a reality. This brings a range of opportunities – for example, blockchain can track a commodity like a coffee bean from grower to Starbucks consumer, ensuring transparency, fair payment, safety and guarding against forced labour. But the procurement function is also dealing with risks connected with digital, such as cyber security, data and GDPR etc. Like all industries, there is a need for digital skills, and demand outstrips supply. And much like HR, debate rages over the automation of roles at the bottom end of the profession.

2 In your opinion, where is the biggest opportunity for HR professionals to get involved and how can they add value?

In my opinion, collaboration across all business functions is necessary for success in a highly competitive world - silos are not an option. Key areas for HR are:

Talent: procurement/supply are struggling to hire good people. According to the latest CIPS/Hays Procurement Salary Guide, 56 per cent of procurement hiring managers are struggling to find talent. HR can partner more effectively with their colleagues in procurement to help them find the right people – soft skills are becoming increas-ingly important and prized over technical skills, for example.

Skills: can you help upskill the supply function to deal with a more digital future, and move from transactional to strategic? If jobs at the bottom are going to become automated, how will people be reskilled and redeployed? Your CPO (chief procurement officer) will need support here.

Contingent workforces and the freelance economy: a study by Deloitte has found some large companies estimate up to 30 per cent of their procurement spend goes towards contingent workers. Procurement and HR should be collaborating more effectively on the use of contingent labour in the organization, making sure people are equipped to add value from day one and that relationships with recruitment agencies are as effective as possible. Also, provide good work for contractors. One of the most compelling quotes I have featured in an interview recently came from the chief procurement and supply chain officer at Nationwide. After the collapse of Carillion, Nationwide directly employed those workers in the supply chain who had been employed by the contractor. The CPO said: 'You do not outsource risk. You do not outsource responsibility. You've got to make sure you are doing the right thing.'

Forced labour and modern slavery: work with procurement to ensure supply chains are slavery-free, rather than abdicating responsibility because 'they aren't on the payroll'. Support modern slavery reporting and think about whether policies such as low pay and using zero-hours contracts are contributing towards the risk of forced labour in your supply chain. Could you offer a programme similar to the Coop's Bright Futures initiative to help victims of modern slavery into better lives?

Behavioural change: if procurement's role is to embed a cost-conscious culture across the organization, is there anything HR can do to support through change management and behavioural change strategies? Can you work with your colleagues in supply to help them sell their message and to make sure they understand human behaviour?

3 If an HR professional wanted to find out more about supply chain issues, where is the best place for them to start?

Network internally – go and talk to your procurement and supply teams and encourage cross-functional collaboration.

CIPS is the procurement professional body and provides a wealth of information.

Supply Management is the official magazine of the CIPS and the best source of news, analysis and insight on procurement and supply globally.

Read widely – general news publications like the *Economist* feature supply chain-related news, and will give a good sense of how global forces converge and impact business and supply chains.

Conclusion

It can be all too easy for HR professionals to pay lip service to 'product' within the businesses they operate in and not grasp the real opportunity offered by product awareness. In most cases information is readily available and accessible when requested. A simple process of networking and building contacts across the business can enable this. Through enhanced knowledge, HR professionals can then target their actions more effectively and contribute in a more directly commercial way to the benefit of the organization.

Toolkit essentials: 5 steps to improving your product knowledge

1 Find out what are the most profitable products or services provided by your company.

2 Ensure you are providing support to aid in the product lifecycle for these items. Target your activity for maximum commercial impact.

3 Map out the 'people' hubs in your company's wider supply chain. Establish if your expertise can be used to add value in this area.

4 Read the trade press and look out for examples of innovation and results from competitors.

5 With support from key stakeholders in the business map out the product lifecycle so you can utilize it to provide context for new recruits and to target HR interventions.

Questions for reflection

Q. Who are the key people involved in managing supply chain issues for your business? Have you connected with them recently to review current trends and issues?

Q. Are you familiar with your company's statement in relation to the Modern Slavery Act?

Q. What would your communication be to your business if it encountered supply chain issues to the extent where 80 per cent of your business locations had to close? What would be your guidance to employees in affected locations? What's your stance on whether they would still be paid?

References

Armstrong, A (2017) Leicester factories 'ticking time bomb' as Asos and New Look join lobbying forces, *Telegraph*, 19 August, available from: www.telegraph.co.uk/business/2017/08/19/leicester-factories-ticking-time-bomb-asos-new-look-join-lobbying/ [accessed 12 April 2018]

Gorepatti, K (2016) Zara's agile supply chain is the source of its competitive advantage, *Digitalist*, 30 March, available from: www.digitalistmag.com/digital-supply-networks/2016/03/30/zaras-agile-supply-chain-is-source-of-competitive-advantage-04083335 [accessed 12 April 2018]

O'Marah, K (2018) 3 supply chain lessons from the KFC Fowl-Up, *Forbes*, 1 March, available from: www.forbes.com/sites/kevinomarah/2018/03/01/three-supply-chain-lessons-from-the-kfc-fowl-up/#57600dbc1cb1 [accessed 12 April 2018]

People and culture 09

Introduction

In this chapter our focus will be on people and culture, specifically how this maps out in the business you work in. We will look at the concept of 'People Experience' as opposed to 'Human Resources' and identify ways in which you can create and support a healthy culture within the organization.

How things get done

In most businesses it's likely that processes and procedures are well mapped out and guidelines issued where relevant in relation to how things should be done. The reality, however, is that it will be the unwritten rules and processes that will be the ones that people will follow and which will generate action and momentum. Think of this from an HR practitioner perspective and in relation to the processes and procedures that typically originate from our function. It is of course a given that stakeholders should be engaged in the process of creating such work and where this happens it's true that you will stand a greater chance of success in creating meaningful work. However, if you can engage the deeper narrative of the unspoken rules and influencers, much more can be achieved with less effort and improved credibility. To an extent we are looking at organizational politics here along with the impact and power of key influencers in your business. These people may or may not be the ones at the top of the organizational hierarchy and their impact should never be underestimated. These are the people who could be your most persistent blockers and disruptors but if engaged with respect in the right way will become your biggest advocates and champions for progressive HR. So how do you engage with this deeper narrative? Slowly and mindfully in a natural and authentic way. This is something that it really is worth spending time on in order to achieve sustained results and create meaningful relationships. It's important to note that this level of connection requires the HR professional to be present daily and deploy the skills identified in the 'networking' chapter in Part One of this book. It needs to be embedded as an ongoing way of working as opposed to a 'project' or 'initiative'.

People Experience (PX)

PX is what's happening in your business right now; it's what every person is experiencing on a day-to-day basis and the framework through which organizational culture is created. As indicated in the introduction of this book it is useful to consider a model for PX where the experience is supported by four pillars:

- the happiness and wellbeing of people;
- smart use of data and technology;
- commercial and evidence-based action;
- reflective of factors influencing the future of work.

These four elements combined, enabled by Agile project management, determine the success or failure of 'people' interventions within a business. We'll look at Agile in the context of HR and explore the PX model further in Part Four of this book.

Figure 9.1 PX model

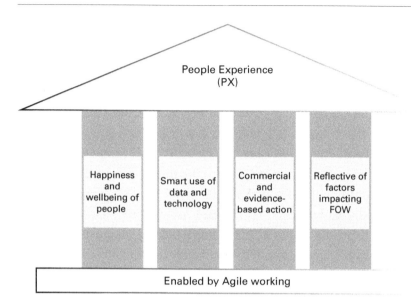

In considering the above, HR practitioners should be aware of their own thought processes surrounding delivery of action. It can be common to start from a point of 'what' should be delivered but in this approach key information is missed. If we approach work from an 'experience first' perspective we start with 'why' and look at the reasons why specific action is needed. Then we move on to look at what impact that piece of work has on the 'experience' of people within the organization.

To quote Simon Sinek, people don't buy 'what' you do, they buy 'why' you do it (Sinek, 2016). Individuals outside of the HR function won't necessarily buy into the end product of what you deliver but if you connect it with why you're delivering it in relation to the experience you want to provide for them it's a whole different story.

If every day we focus on improving the experience of work for people working within an organization, culture shift occurs and performance measures improve.

As an example of how this works in practice I refer to the 'experience' of annual appraisals. During my time as HR Director at River Island we completely rebooted appraisals and instead of focusing on the 'process' we switched to focusing on the 'experience' of the people on the receiving end of it. At the point of instigating the change it was clear that the traditional process wasn't working. The completion rate for appraisals was incredibly poor and feedback was that it wasn't the right fit for the business, there didn't seem to be any commercial argument to support retaining it, and in fact the commercial argument to ditch the appraisal process was stronger in relation to the number of hours lost balanced with the return on it. For individuals, they didn't see much value in it either as it wasn't connected to pay increments and often promotion decisions were made that didn't correlate with the feedback in the appraisal. So, we knew that the 'experience' for the end users wasn't great and there was nothing productive arising from HR taking the position of 'HR police' to drive completion and tick boxes for a process that wasn't adding value.

We then took the information we had, eg statistics showing that completion rates were low – in fact in 2014 only 7 per cent of appraisals were returned in the head office environment – and combined it with end user feedback. We brought this together with information we were seeing externally at the time about organizations ditching the appraisal process and decided to do the same. One such example of this is an article from PwC which refers to the importance of 'Equipping managers with the appropriate skills to deliver effective and motivational performance conversations on an ongoing basis and creating a culture where employees can grow and develop' (PwC, 2015).

In real terms this meant that the annual appraisal was gone and had been replaced by an employee-led process whereby an employee could request a 'development review' with their line manager when they felt ready for it, not at a specific time of the year determined by anyone else. So we put ownership for personal development in the hands of the people to whom it mattered most. In addition, we promoted a culture of real-time feedback and meaningful conversations between managers and their teams. We encouraged managers to ensure that at all times people within their teams were aware of the overall goals of the business and for the area they were working in, and also to ensure that all individuals knew what they were personally accountable for. We supported managers with finding the right channels and ways to do that for their area of the business and consciously pushed the idea of 'in the moment' feedback so people knew at all times how they were doing.

Sure there were teething problems and hiccups along the way, but a couple of years on from embedding the change the results started to become clear. Engagement metrics showed that the business was up 6 per cent on the perception of management, 3 per cent on leadership and up 1 per cent on personal growth. Overall engagement increased 2 per cent to sit at 81 per cent. One particularly interesting measure related to a manager giving positive feedback to help employees improve performance and their career uplifted by 9 per cent as a result of the change and the supporting L&D programme. There was also a 6 per cent uplift on the measure linked to 'my manager makes time for me and supports me to do my job well'. All in all a great result for switching the focus to 'experience' over process.

Environment

When we think in terms of 'experience' and how this impacts on performance it can be helpful to look at the environment that individuals work in.

Writing for *Forbes* in December 2015, Jacob Morgan makes reference to Gensler's Workplace Index study which suggests that four key areas need to be available for individuals in a working environment in order to enable peak performance. Specifically, it suggests that people need an area where they can focus, they need an area for collaboration with colleagues, an area or environment for learning, and finally an area to socialize. The suggestion is that if a working environment provides designated spaces for these activities individuals are more likely to be able to perform (Morgan, 2015).

Therefore, this definitely needs to be taken into consideration if we are to enable high performance. Something else to consider in relation to this is the growing research highlighting the downsides of open plan offices. One article from January 2018, makes reference to a study from CTF, Service Research Centre at Karlstad University, Sweden, which highlights that 'the more co-workers that share a space, the less satisfied the employees are' (Phys.org, 2018).

Talent acquisition

In relation to talent acquisition, the focus on experience needs to start at the pre-hire stage and it will then progress through to onboarding or regret depending on the success of the application. For talent acquisition, it's possible to apply an 'engagement funnel' approach to assist in targeting activity at each level.

At the entry point of the funnel our strategic focus is directed to a vast group of people, some of whom will be the target candidates and some of whom will not. At this level, we should be seeking to provide an experience that attracts and engages the right people in the right way whilst at the same time maintaining a professional and credible relationship with the other candidates who may well be our commercial customers or candidates with skills suitable for future roles. Examples of experiential activities to consider at this level could be as follows:

Figure 9.2   Example of an engagement funnel for talent acquisition

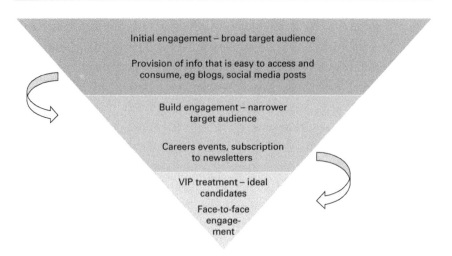

- company blog;
- social media content;
- advertisements;

As individuals engage with the above it's then likely that they will progress further into the funnel and a different type of experience will be required in order to maintain engagement. For example:

- careers events;
- subscription to newsletter updates;
- CV or profile review;
- alumni events and community.

Then we progress to the exit point of the funnel where the pool of people has been narrowed to the point of selection and the experience to be delivered needs to be personal and engaging, specifically targeted to that individual and the role they have applied for:

- provision of additional information to the candidate including company and role info;
- face-to-face interview;
- personal feedback on interview;
- after-care and management of relationship post interview;

Activity 5

Map out the talent acquisition experience funnel for your business.

Conclusion

One of the biggest stumbling blocks for any HR professional can be underestimating the impact of people and culture in relation to People Experience. There are so many factors that combine here that if not handled correctly can derail HR activity and reputation.

It's not enough to know who's who in a business; it is essential to invest energy in cultivating relationships with key decision makers and influencers. Think about the obvious ones and the not-so-obvious ones too. With key influencers identified it's then possible to facilitate meaningful change through shifting your focus to looking at the experience that you want to provide as opposed to putting process first.

Toolkit essentials: 5 steps to enabling people to perform at their best

1 Tap into the unwritten narrative of the organization you are working in in order to remain connected to the truth of 'how things get done'.

2 Build credible relationships with key influencers and decision makers.

3 Establish working practices that provide exceptional experiences for the people within the business.

4 Review your talent acquisition strategy to ensure consistency of experience through from first contact to onboarding or regret.

5 Release work to enhance the experience in small increments made up of practical and useable solutions. Test theories, listen to feedback, adapt and then go again.

Questions for reflection

Q. Who are the real decision makers in your organization and how can you improve your relationships with them?

Q. How does the experience you provide for the people working in your organization compare to the experience provided to customers of the organization?

Q. What one thing can you do today to improve the experience of people working within your business?

Q. Is your working environment set up to support and deliver a quality of employee experience that will support and enable peak performance?

References

Morgan, J (2015) How the physical workspace impacts the employee experience, *Forbes*, available at: https://www.forbes.com/sites/jacobmorgan/2015/12/03/how-the-physical-workspace-impacts-the-employee-experience/#bf42c3a779ea [accessed 2 August 2018]

Phys.org. (2018) Employees who work in open-plan offices feel worse and are more dissatisfied with their work, available at: https://phys.org/news/2018-01-employees-open-plan-offices-worse-dissatisfied.html [accessed 2 August 2018]

PwC (2015) More companies planning to ditch annual performance reviews and ratings, but will employees benefit? Available at: http://pwc.blogs.com/press_room/2015/07/more-companies-planning-to-ditch-end-of-annual-performance-reviews-and-ratings-but-will-employees-be.html [accessed 2 August 2018]

Sinek, S (2016) *Start with Why*, Joosr Ltd

Productivity 10

Introduction

In this chapter our focus will be on the topic of productivity and we will consider what role HR professionals could and should be playing with regards to this. Productivity is a key determining factor in the success of any organization and the actions of individuals working within HR can have a direct impact on this, ranging from the impact of setting and implementing wage levels to workforce planning and embedding effective learning and development interventions. As observed in the book *Organizational Linkages: Understanding the productivity paradox*, 'individual productivity is often measured only against labor input, and labor may be counted in a number of different ways.' Then, 'At the organizational level, a total factor approach is often used, that is, inputs consist of labor, materials, capital, and energy' (Harris, 1994).

How will this chapter shape my thinking?

- It will help you gain a deeper understanding of how productivity is measured in your organization.
- It will encourage you to think about the impact your actions have on productivity.
- It will provide you with some ideas for how you could contribute to improved productivity in the business you work in.

What is productivity?

Writing for the *Independent* in October 2017, Ben Chu describes productivity as 'the amount of work produced either per worker or per hour worked' (Chu, 2017). It's also a measure recorded by the Office for National Statistics on a quarterly basis. Productivity can be considered on a local or 'business' level and also in the context of the wider economy where 'Gross Domestic Product' is identified as the measure for the total value of goods and services produced in a country in one year. In his article, Chu observes that in the UK productivity has 'flatlined' since the final quarter of 2007, with it being no higher in the final quarter of 2017 than it was 10 years prior – an astonishing fact when you consider the rate of technology advancements in the same period. Chu then moves on to explore what that means for wages and notes that the result of flat productivity is that it is difficult to raise wages; he observes a direct connection between flat productivity and that wages in 2017 were also at a 10-year low point.

An important point for all HR professionals is to understand how productivity is defined in the organization they work in. In some cases this will be more obvious than in others; for example, in a manufacturing or distribution environment there will be some clear identifiers, eg units processed per hour, or rate of output for a product line. However, in other sectors 'productivity' can be harder to define and can seem at odds with the nature of the business. For example, in creative industries the output can be more subjective and measures to drive productivity could potentially impact negatively on the creative nature of the work.

How is it measured?

When you have an understanding of how productivity is defined in the organization you work in you can then establish how it is measured and look at trends that have emerged over time. For most businesses this will be an ever-evolving process directly linked to efficiency measures but it can still be common for 'business as usual' to mask opportunities for further improvement. In light of this it can be useful for organizations to commission a review through engaging an external partner. One example of a specialist partner for this is ReThink Productivity, who have provided the following case study demonstrating how this might work in practice.

CASE STUDY   ReThink Productivity

The background

This case study relates to a retail business operating with 390 stores across three different formats. The retailer engaged ReThink Productivity as they wanted to make improvements across the business in order to improve commercial results.

The retailer had not measured how long activities took to rebase the number of hours they needed in each store for a significant period of time. They thought their cost base was too high compared to the actual workload and there was a commercial drive to reduce costs to at least offset the upward cost pressures of minimum wage, the apprenticeship levy and pension changes.

In addition to a mismatch of hours available to workload, the ratio of management hours to colleague hours was high and there was little consistency in the number of managers and management roles in place between stores. The leadership structure in each store had tended to evolve over time, as had the number of types of management roles in place.

The challenge

The retailer wanted to reduce their management costs overall while maintaining cover for their extended trading hours and ensuring leadership for customer service. They wanted more consistency between stores and a robust evidence basis for any changes they proposed. They engaged ReThink to measure activity undertaken by managers in a range of stores with different formats and sales turnovers and then use the resulting analysis to suggest options for new management models for stores.

What happened?

An activity study was conducted in a selection of stores that quantified how different manager roles spent their time. Specialist analysts completed 'Day in the Life of' studies by following a manager for a day, documenting what they did and using British Pace Rating standards to identify if work was undertaken at a faster or slower pace than 'swift and business-like'. The study produced data that categorized activities as value adding, essential tasks, or non-value adding or wasted.

Analysis of the collected data showed that:

- There was a significant variance in how management roles spent their time in store – by role and by store.
- Many of the management roles overlapped in what they did – best practice suggests that management roles are most effective when they have a clear purpose and defined accountabilities.
- Managers were spending a significant amount of time carrying out non-managerial and non-value-adding activities. This confirmed the view that there were more management hours than needed in the store.

ReThink then used the analysis to propose three different structure options based on:

- defined span of control for each manager (how many heads can a manager effectively lead?);
- cover for all trading hours – taking in to account extended hours and holiday times;
- defined roles underpinned by clear objectives to facilitate role clarification as part of any changes made.

The recommendations were validated using the management study data. The data was also used to create the business case for change within the business and for consultation meetings with managers.

The outcome

The retailer was able to review and revise both the rules underpinning the three options ReThink recommended and the scenarios themselves. Linking this review to a simple model that showed the ongoing costs for each of the future structure options and modelled the potential impact of changes, this information enabled the client to have evidence-based discussions with their stakeholders and define their optimum solution.

The new management structure has been successfully implemented, supported by a clear business rationale and role-clarification work to create more consistent management roles across the business.

Variances between stores have been addressed, providing a better match of colleague hours available to the workload demands of each store, supported by a more consistent management structure across stores.

The impact of this type of review can be significant, with reported productivity opportunities identified by ReThink as follows:

- department store – £10 million;
- homeware retailer – £6 million;
- fashion retailer – £2.5 million;
- coffee shop +25 per cent more coffees made per colleague;
- discounter – £14 million.

Simon Hedaux, Managing Director at ReThink Productivity, advises that the first step in identifying effective measures of productivity is to look for what data is currently available and use this to form an evidence trail and make a KPI. He observes that there is no one killer stat that organizations should focus on here and that any data can be used for this purpose. From a 'people' perspective it can be interesting to look at engagement survey results and specifically at responses linked to how people feel about the variety of their work and their place of work. Simon highlights specifically that a common theme uncovered through his work is a link between employees who are dissatisfied with the variety of their work and overall productivity for the area they work in.

How can productivity be improved?

Based on his experience of supporting multiple organizations, Hedaux has some clear views on how organizations can improve performance in this area.

Listen. He points out that it is important to listen to the voices of individuals carrying out the work and also ask them for suggestions for how things could be done more effectively.

Inconsistency. Hedaux observes that he often uncovers inconsistencies in working practices and that these are typically the things that lie at the root of low productivity. One example is a significant inconsistency of break times across a retailer, which also linked to a massive variation in how store managers were spending their time across multiple locations, most tapping into their personal operating preference with their balance of off-floor and on-floor activity. He also noted a lack of consistency with regard to 'training' and observes that it is very rare for any 'training' activity to be recorded when they go in and do their initial review and assessment work. Hedaux feels this links directly back to low productivity, as neglecting this results in individuals not being able to perform to the best of their abilities. Essentially, by not having effective and consistent L&D programmes, employees' opportunities for development and increased productivity are compromised.

Focus on the customer. A surprising fact to come from Hedaux's work is the discovery that for a typical retail business, less than 20 per cent of a store employees' time will be spent on customer-focused activity. The weight of time is instead spent on tasks such as putting stock out – an interesting point when you consider that most retailers promote the concept of 'customer first'. In addition, a great point to start with productivity improvements is through adoption of technology and infrastructure to support 'tasking' in this environment.

Be in it for the long term. Hedaux observes that he often comes across organizations that view a productivity review as a one-off project or initiative, the aim being to cut costs at a specific point in time. He notes that this short-term approach rarely offers sustained results and in effect will result in further problems down the line. His advice is to view this as an ongoing journey in order to achieve sustained results.

Get involved. It's interesting to note that Hedaux states that it is rare for him to see any representation from HR around the table when he goes into a business to consult or pitch for work. In most cases the work is being commissioned by an Operations function or by Finance. He observes that this is a bit of a missed opportunity and a potential risk as the focus is then defined in a very specific way. He notes that Finance's main objective is to cut costs, sometimes without understanding the long-term implications of this and the operations functions often seem to have the motive of needing to prove 'Finance' wrong! He observes that HR can bring a different slant to the conversation and ensure the focus is on the best deployment of people through engaging them in meaningful work. It's then possible to effectively consider organizational structures, spans of control, the budget for learning and development and the employees' voice in any measures to improve productivity.

Conclusion

The productivity of an organization is an absolute key factor in determining the success of the business. All too often it can be considered to fall outside of the remit of HR, or HR professionals are hesitant to get involved. There is an important role to play here to ensure a balanced approach to reviewing and responding to productivity measures and in particular a key role for HR professionals to ensure that employee engagement is considered and that the employee voice is heard. It doesn't need to be difficult to make a real impact in this area either. From the case study we see that simple factors such as listening to the people, investigating and understanding why inconsistencies in process may exist across multiple locations, and ensuring a focus on the customer all have a role to play.

Toolkit essentials: 5 steps to improve productivity in your business

1 Get involved in the conversation, balancing the views of finance and operations with your own perspective and professional insight.

2 Ensure you have clarity over how productivity is defined and measured in different areas within your business.

3 Review and refresh skills training and hubs to ensure the appropriate balance of quality and speed.

4 Ensure that you stay close enough to the reality of business operations so you can spot trends evolving that may impact on productivity, for example inconsistent application of practices which are assumed to be in place.

5 Ensure that 'productivity' is considered as an ongoing journey as opposed to an initiative to reduce costs at a particular point in time.

Questions for reflection

Q. In what areas of your business is creativity actively measured and *how* is it measured?

Q. How are trends in productivity recorded in your business and what are your observations on this over an extended time period?

Q. What is the area of lowest productivity in your organization and what action could you take to support improvements in this area?

References

Chu, B (2017) What is productivity? And why does it matter that it's falling again? *Independent*, 6 October, available from: www.independent.co.uk/news/business/analysis-and-features/productivity-what-is-it-meaning-define-uk-economy-explained-a7986781.html [accessed 15 April 2018]

Harris, D (1994) *Organizational Linkages*, National Academy Press, Washington DC

Annual results 11

Introduction

In this chapter our focus will be on 'annual results' and we will look at the importance of this in the context of your own business and competitor organizations. We will highlight the key elements that HR professionals should be aware of and promote a concept of shared ownership that will enable you to contribute at a more strategic level in relation to this.

How will this chapter shape my thinking?

- It will give you a starting point from which you can begin to interpret the annual results of your company and other organizations.
- It will help to improve your confidence when discussing annual results at a strategic level.
- It will prompt you to get involved in contributing to the annual results and helping to shape the narrative around the figures to be published.

What are they?

The annual report and accounts can be defined as 'The report issued annually to shareholders containing the directors' report, the auditor's report and the financial statements for the year' (Rice, 2011).

In essence, it is a document that reports on the company's activities and financial performance for the year preceding their publication. The audience is typically shareholders and other interested parties who wish to find out more about the trading performance and operating arrangements within the business.

Elements typically found within the annual reports are as follows:

- financial highlights;
- statement from the chairman and CEO;
- overview of business proposition;
- info on potential new business options;
- key performance indicators for the business;
- overview of risks and mitigating factors;
- information on the board of directors and operating board;
- corporate governance statement;
- information on corporate social responsibility;
- information relating to the audit committee or processes;
- directors' remuneration report;
- income statement;
- balance sheet;
- cash flow statement;
- information relating to equity and shareholders;
- notes and other disclosures relating to the information presented.

The annual statutory accounts are essentially consolidated monthly management accounts.

The Management Accounts are produced by the business to track performance against Target and Prior Year on a monthly basis. Your Finance Business Partners will be able to provide monthly/quarterly updates in real time, with the context of how business performance is tracking against expectation, ie Budget/Target; it's important to note that the Management Accounts go into much more detail than the statutory accounts.

Where to find them

It should in theory be a very simple process for you to obtain the company results for the business you work in. As a starting point, look to leverage the networking skills built in previous chapters and open a discussion around the annual results with a key influencer working in Finance. Just ask if it's possible for you to have a copy of the last published results, explaining that you're looking to broaden your awareness of this. Consider arranging a time for the relevant person to talk you through the results so that you have the 'in-house' interpretation and understanding of how they have been put together. It's this narrative that you can then build on to shape your thinking and to ensure that the work you do is relevant and commercial. For example, 'If I implement this initiative now, what impact might be seen in the next set of published results? How can I ensure the work I do has impact in the right areas?'

In addition, in the UK, it is also possible to obtain copies of published results from Companies House and a simple web search can enable this. This can be a particularly useful thing to do if you are considering applying for a role with a particular business and you would like to do an extra layer of preparation prior to an interview. In some cases, it may make you rethink your application altogether. For large companies it's also possible to find their annual report on their website.

Another good source of information relating to the annual accounts of your own business and competitor businesses can be the trade press. Certainly, for larger organizations, it can become a bit of an event, with the media actively waiting for the information and then assessing the implications of the results on the wider market and outlook for the business.

What to look for and reviewing trends

Before getting into the detail of what to look for in the annual results it's important to remember that they are only ever going to be a snapshot in time and frustratingly it can be that we as HR professionals don't see this 'snapshot' until the information is potentially out of date and the window for positive impact has passed. This is one of the reasons that it is so important to make meaningful connections with your colleagues in Finance and ensure you are part of the discussions around trends throughout the year and not just in a position where you are reviewing what happened after the results have been posted. I would encourage you to seek monthly and quarterly updates from your Finance Business Partner to stay relevant here.

Tom Ormond, Head of Finance at Powerleague Group, notes that it's important to remember that the statutory accounts have to be submitted to Companies House nine months after the company's financial year end; many organizations leave it too close to the deadline due to the resource involved in preparing the accounts, but also to prevent sensitive information entering the market until it's out of date.

Ormond goes on to advise that another point to look out for in complex group structures, especially those involving operations in multiple markets or hybrid ownership structures, is that there will often be debt arrangements between group companies put in place to be tax efficient. To the non-financial eye this may mean that results appear better or worse than expected; for example a company may appear loss-making due to the interest it pays on a debt to a parent company. This is not a bad thing, it just needs to be considered. For example, many companies in the news recently (Amazon, Starbucks) do not make a profit in the UK so as to avoid paying tax – they instead pay large amounts of interest to group companies based in low-tax-regime countries.

The annual statutory accounts will contain several pages of notes relating the income statement and balance sheet – it's key to read these notes in order to provide context to the financial statements, specifically any change year on year. In addition, when reviewing competitors' accounts it's also very important to check any supplementary notes as they can reveal additional facts in relation to both what is said and what is not.

All publicly quoted companies (listed on the stock exchange) and many larger privately owned companies will also report on corporate social responsibility and carbon usage – this provides a good insight into the company, its ethics and culture. In addition, the UK Government has announced that under the Companies Act 2006 (Strategic and Directors' Reports) Regulations 2013, quoted companies are required to report their annual greenhouse gas (GHG) emissions in their directors' report. Carbon reporting is the first vital step for companies to make reductions in emissions. By measuring and reporting GHG emissions companies can begin to set targets and put in place carbon management initiatives to reduce emissions in the future. Defra (the UK Department for Environment, Food and Rural Affairs) has estimated that reporting will contribute to saving four million tonnes of CO_2e emissions by 2021.

How can HR professionals contribute to them?

As you become more familiar with the format of the accounts for the business you work in you should find that you are better placed to make a contribution not only to the narrative of the accounts but also to the commercial impact that you and your function have.

As noted by Tom Ormond, the absolute key here is to build a great relationship with your Finance Business Partner and ensure that you meet regularly for updates. Specifically, make sure that you understand how the company is performing against budget/target as this is the yardstick against which the board and management team set objectives. The annual accounts will only contain a comparison to the prior financial year, not the internal targets set by the business, so it's also important that you are absolutely clear on what the targets are.

As you gain credibility and through regular contact with your Finance Business Partner you will then naturally find yourself in a position whereby you can assist in shaping the narrative for the published accounts. Then to follow this you can support in the narrative around the communication of the results within the business to support and drive employee engagement.

Through signing up to regular news alerts – eg Google New Alerts and the London Stock Exchange's Regulatory News Service (RNS) – you will also gain additional insight into the market, your competitors and how the external world views your company. You can then utilize this information to enable you to participate actively in discussions around company performance and expand the scope of your contribution beyond a standard 'HR' remit.

Conclusion

Don't wait until the annual accounts are produced to see them; ask your Finance Business Partner for regular performance updates, which will help your understanding of the company performance in real time. Ensure you understand how the process works in your business. Identify key competitors, especially if they are a PLC listed on the stock exchange as they have to publish regular updates to the market including announcements via the RNS of anything 'material'. Sign up to the London Stock Exchange and get on the e-mail distribution list of these RNS announcements. It's also important to be clear on the ownership structure of your business. Is it listed on the stock exchange and therefore owned by shareholders? Is it privately owned? Is it owned by a private equity house which will be looking to grow and sell it? How much debt does the business have with financial institutions? Also, don't assume that all debt is bad; debt can be good for business as it's an efficient source of funding but, as with a mortgage, only if the business can afford the repayments (interest and or capital). As an HR professional look for how you can get involved in the narrative that supports the accounts, how can you contribute to this and how can you shape it. Ensure that through working with your Finance partners you are seeing the true picture of performance and through that you are then targeting HR activities effectively to really support the business you are operating in.

Toolkit essentials: 5 steps to enhance your strategic impact in relation to annual results

1 Ensure you are familiar with your company's annual results and liaise with a contact in Finance to ensure you understand the reporting format and key messages.

2 Track back over the past three years of results for your company and identify trends and themes that may still be having an impact on results.

3 Identify key competitors and obtain copies of their annual reports; note when they are due to publish so you can keep track of industry trends and competitor activity.

4 Consider how the work you are delivering could be referenced in the company's annual report. Are you able to link HR activity to commercial impact? Are you working on the right things and at the right level?

5 Become familiar with the process for how the annual reports are created. What is the time line? When and how can you contribute to the narrative?

Questions for reflection

Q. How are your annual results communicated to employees within your business? What role can you play in this in relation to employee engagement?

Q. Who is your key contact in Finance that you can work alongside in relation to this?

Q. How can you target your HR activity in such a way that it makes a positive impact on the annual results?

Reference

Rice, A (2011) *Accounts Demystified*, Pearson, Harlow, p220

Commercial focus   12

Introduction

In this chapter our focus will be on enhancing our commercial focus and looking at how we can shift our mindset to ensure that commerciality becomes an intrinsic part of who we are and how we operate. I'll also share some of the personal strategies that I deployed in order to take my vision of a personal styling service from notes on a sheet of A4 paper to becoming a commercial venture operating in a number of retail stores.

How will this chapter shape my thinking?

- It will encourage you to be more commercial in all aspects of what you do.
- It will support you in broadening your remit beyond the scope of HR.
- It will encourage you to identify commercial opportunities early.
- It will enhance your confidence so that you feel able to act decisively when commercial opportunities arise.

Consistency

Commerciality is a trait that needs to be applied consistently in all areas of what you do, both at work and outside of it. It needs to become an embedded habit and a core component of how you operate. Start with reviewing how you manage and plan your own finances outside of work and challenge yourself to become more commercial with regards to how you do this. Look at your overheads and your balance of income over expenditure on a month-by-month basis. Consider if you can reduce your personal expenditure and take steps to ensure that your cash is in the best place, maximizing any opportunities for interest or profit. Viewing your own financial situation in a more professional way provides a foundation from which you are better placed to develop and leverage commercial focus in a corporate environment.

Revenue streams

One of the first things to consider in the context of the business you work in is to clearly identify all of the different revenue streams of the business. Where do the sales come from? It's certainly worth investing some time with your contact in Finance to review this. You could look at this in terms of product or service lines and identify which are the most profitable. You can also look at the channels of revenue and identify where the customer base is, for example a trading location or geography, online, mobile, through social media etc. You can then reflect on how you are currently supporting those functions within the business from an HR perspective and look to deploy strategies to strengthen these business areas, for example in the areas of talent acquisition and retention. From this you can also start to shape your thinking around future talent planning and organizational design in relation to any potential areas of declining sales and shifts in consumer behaviour.

In addition, through building your knowledge of existing revenue streams you will eventually create a map of the organization for yourself that might help you spot a commercial opportunity that you could go on to take forward.

CASE STUDY   Style Studio at River Island

During my time at River Island, in addition to maintaining my remit as HR Director I also founded a commercial venture which went on to operate in a number of the flagship retail stores.

The venture was called Style Studio and is in essence a complimentary personal styling service for customers. In this case study I share with you the process I followed in order to create and launch that venture.

At the point where I first proposed the venture to our CEO, I had been in the business for just over two years and was therefore fairly well established in my role as HR Director. I had already strengthened the HR function to a position where it was actively supporting the business and things were progressing well. And this is a key point. If you want to explore the option of creating a commercial venture outside of your existing role you need to be 100 per cent certain that you and your team are performing or even outperforming in getting the day job done. If there are any questions surrounding the current performance of your function it's unlikely that you will get the backing you need in order to pursue other ventures.

Now by this point I had a really good understanding of the business; I understood the revenue streams of the business and had a good understanding of the core customer. I had a good internal network and was actively spending time in the business talking to people at all levels, getting a good understanding of issues and opportunities. I also had a clear understanding of the business strategy as well as a good connection with my CEO and a good understanding of how he personally liked to see things done.

I'll be clear that at this point in time I was immersed in the business and it was a business I loved and felt passionate about. I loved the fashion retail world and not only was I employed by River Island, I was a genuine customer too. I was totally engaged, living and breathing every part of being in that business. As a result of this passion and connection I was able to spot an opportunity for a service that didn't exist in the business at that time. I realized that there was scope to add an additional service that would not only be revenue generating but it would also be brand building too. I had the first vision for the styling service and I felt fired up and excited about it.

At this point the next step for me was just to start the process of floating the idea and I tested it out with a few people in different parts of the business. The responses were mixed but overall pretty positive. It was also at this point that I first floated the idea with my CEO too, just in a very subtle way, saying it would be great if we had something like that. This was an important step for me because I wanted to get the conversation stated in a very non-pressured way whilst I was subtly collecting wider views and opinions and starting the process of building my business case.

One of the pieces of feedback I received was that the business had tried something similar a number of years previously and it had failed. I then knew I needed to research what had happened in this scenario as it would certainly be raised again further down the line. As it turned out, the previous venture had been set up in just one store in Ireland and had been fully run and operated by the retail team in that store who also had all of their existing duties to perform at the same time. In learning this I became more confident that what I was thinking about was very different and I was confident that the failure of the previous styling service wouldn't impact on my ability to demonstrate the commercial viability of the new one.

Next came the research because I knew I would need facts behind me to build the business case. I investigated all of the existing options for similar services and compared the benefits of each one. I actively went to experience the services provided so I had first-hand knowledge of this and could subtly talk to the stylists to get additional insights into how the services operated. This helped me shape the overall vision and positioning for the service. My vision was that I wanted to create an experience for the customer that felt like the premium service you would get from a 1:1 appointment with a personal stylist but then make it accessible on the high street and for all River Island customers. In addition, I wanted the potential to introduce add-on services and build the idea over time with things like hosting parties and events in the space, going on to look at providing paid-for training courses for stylists further down the line.

From this, I then moved on to map out a very basic financial projection for what I thought the service could generate in terms of revenue. I came at this from the point of thinking about how many items a customer would typically purchase in a styling session and then working that through into average costs. I looked at average transaction values in a typical store and came up with a projected increase on that. What I was also clear on was that this needed to be a complimentary service; the revenue would come from the increase in transaction value through the customer purchasing more items.

By this point I had progressed my conversations with my CEO and had shared some of my research with him. It was becoming more normal for us to have conversations about this. I was also keeping the conversation alive with other key stakeholders in the business and being open about sharing my thoughts and ideas. I was, in essence, getting people comfortable with the idea.

After talking to our COO about the idea I then called in some support from a contact in Finance who helped me map out my initial workings into a draft budget for the venture. They were also able to help in mapping in some costs too and again I also drew on my contacts in other business areas to support with this. Retail, Visual Merchandising, Shopfitting and Shop Planning all had valuable information and insights that I needed to incorporate.

I finally got to a position where I had a credible business case that I could present to the CEO. I'd like to say that it got accepted straight away but of course it didn't. I needed to go back and rework it and also obtain information and evidence to demonstrate that I had the ability and capacity to do this without any risk to the HR function. At this point in time I was investing a lot of my personal time and personal financial resources into research and planning, consistently working late into the evening following my passion and vision to get this done. I was throwing my heart and soul into it because I believed in it so strongly and because I genuinely believed it was a service our customers wanted and would love. I knew this would be a success and I knew revenue and great PR opportunities for the business would be gained as a result of it.

There were several further knock-backs and push-backs along the way but I was undeterred and kept taking the feedback and readjusting until the case was so compelling it received the go-ahead. This is where it became so important that I had picked a venture I really believed in. I was prepared to fight for it because I knew it was the right thing to do. I was listening and learning all the time and my initial contacts that I had floated the idea with were becoming allies who were backing me if they were asked for their opinion on it.

Then, eventually, I was given the go-ahead to proceed and everything got very real. The draft budget became 'the' budget and instead of floating ideas I was organizing project meetings to get the venture off the ground. I needed to collaborate cross-functionally with all business areas from Finance to Technology, Retail, Merchandising, Shopfitting and Design just to name a few, and slowly the project came together.

I started to recruit for the initial team and had to find a way to sell the dream and concept to people who had nothing tangible to look at at the point where I was interviewing them. I'm pleased to say the vision was compelling enough to enable me to secure some absolutely key initial hires, people who would play a significant role in the development of the service and who could bring their expert insight with them to ensure that the venture was a success.

Subsequently, after months of planning and preparation with the team, the first Style Studio was launched in one of the brand's flagship stores on London's Oxford Street, then over time additional locations were added, including Birmingham and Liverpool.

In its first year of operation, over 1,000 customers made use of the service, a figure that then nearly doubled in its second year. In addition, in one location, the average transaction value (ATV) for sales within the Style Studio lounge consistently averaged over 300 per cent more than the standard ATV for that store. This was a real testament to both the quality of service and experience being provided by the Style Studio team and also a reflection on the quality of product available within the business.

Conclusion

Good commercial practice and understanding needs to be reflected in all aspects of how you operate, both at work and outside of it. It is essential to ingrain good habits as standard so that operating from this point of commerciality becomes the normal state for you. Then, through developing your understanding of the business you operate in and ensuring an in-depth knowledge of existing revenue streams, you can then place yourself in a position where you can identify potential new ones. If you do decide to pursue a commercial venture in addition to your day job it will be essential to pick something that you feel a real connection with and are passionate about. You can expect to have to work additional hours and have additional draws on your time and energy to get the project moving. In addition, you need to back your idea to the point where you're prepared to fight for it and prepared to reassess your position, take feedback and continually evolve your plan in order to have it signed off. Setting up a new venture in this way is hard but it's also incredibly rewarding and once established it really does take the concept of commercial HR to a completely different level.

Toolkit essentials: 10 steps to help you develop a commercial venture

1 Ensure you and your team are doing the 'day job' well.

2 Choose something you are personally interested in, something you have a passion for.

3 Establish if anything similar has been implemented before and learn from that.

4 Research competitor activity in this area; experience it first-hand where possible.

5 Create your budget and call in help from allies and experts to support with this.

6 Refine and strengthen your business case and allay all fears and concerns.

7 Get ready to get knocked back and be ready to fight for your idea. Choose something you really believe in.

8 When you get the go-ahead, step up and do what it takes to get the job done.

9 Recruit great people where you need to in order to bring the vision to life.

10 Know that 'done' is never 'done' and continue the process of reviewing and assessing the venture to ensure its continued commercial viability.

Questions for reflection

Q. What is the most profitable product line or service for your business?

Q. How efficiently do you manage your own personal finances?

Q. What commercial opportunity can you identify in your current business?

Q. Who would you need to call on for help in order to get your commercial venture off the ground?

Markets and channels   13

Introduction

In this chapter our focus will be on markets and channels of trade and looking at why enhancing your understanding of these needs to be an essential part of your role. We look at the emerging channels and not only consider the impact of those on customer experience but also map across what they might mean from the perspective of People Experience in your organization as well.

For the purpose of this chapter, 'markets' are defined as the places where the business interacts with its customers or clients in order to sell products. This could be a specific territory or country, or it could be a virtual marketplace. The nature of markets is that they are always changing in response to customer demands and it is therefore imperative to keep up with market trends in order to contribute at a senior level with regards to corporate strategy and planning.

Channels are defined as the medium through which product or services are sold into the markets. For example, one channel could be physical retail stores in the case of a retail business. Another channel could be wholesale, or e-commerce. In addition, we now see the growth of social media channels with product being sold direct to consumers through the likes of Snapchat and Instagram.

How will this chapter shape my thinking?

- This chapter will encourage you to take a holistic view of how customers are serviced through your business and prompt you to identify key markets for growth.

- It will encourage you to keep pace with developments in this area, specifically in relation to research and development of new channels of growth.

- It will encourage you to embrace the unknowns surrounding Brexit and identify key measures to implement in the face of such unknowns.

- It will encourage you to consider the impact of incongruency in relation to the external perception of the business and the internal reality of working in the business.

Omnichannel/multichannel

As a starting point, it's useful to consider what is meant by the term omnichannel and then how this compares to multichannel. *Collins English Dictionary* defines the word 'omni' as meaning 'all, or everywhere'. Multi is defined as 'many, or, more than one'. From this it is then possible to conclude that a business which presents itself as 'omnichannel' is one which operates, or aspires to operate through *all* available channels and a 'multichannel' business as being one that provides products or service through more than one channel.

The optimal position in both scenarios is a desire to provide a consistent customer experience across the whole business and across all channels – not always an easy thing to achieve. However, it is an essential position to aspire to as from a consumer perspective, a consistency of experience and service is very much now expected as the norm.

This is also a point for HR professionals to consider in relation to the experience that is being provided to employees within the business. For example, if services and points of interaction are being provided across multiple channels, eg print, digital, face to face, it is important to establish a consistency of positioning, branding and message in order to build trust and also reflect the DNA of the wider business.

More than ever, employees will be quick to pick up on inauthentic positioning, such as a decision to present the business externally as a leading tech business, or one that is progressive and aspirational, and then have the internal reality be at odds with this, through lack of investment in internal comms and/or technology to facilitate the employee experience.

Global market

The global market is defined as 'The activity of buying or selling goods and services in all the countries of the world, or the value of the goods and services sold' (Financial Times Lexicon, 2018).

Regardless of whether the business you work in trades in the global market or not it is useful to keep yourself up to speed with developments that impact this. From doing this, you will be able to observe trends and factors that may have an indirect knock-on effect on the business you work in, either through rising costs or availability of talented labour.

Brexit

At the time of writing, it is impossible to consider the importance of being aware of markets and channels without mentioning the word Brexit. It's true there are more unknown knowns than there are known knowns at this stage and as such the best course of action would appear to be to keep preparing and working through 'what if' scenarios to test and strengthen business operations in the run-up to it.

As noted by PwC, 'HR has a key role to play in an organization's Brexit journey – from managing the immediate people implications of the referendum vote to business scenario planning.' They then observe three key areas that HR professionals should be focusing on: creating a positive mindset, addressing here-and-now issues, and planning for the longer term (PwC, 2018). So really, at the core of this guidance is a practical common-sense approach that focuses on ensuring stability in the here and now, maintaining an effective dialogue with employees and looking forward in a holistic, proactive way in order to anticipate business impact.

PwC conclude by noting, 'HR has a crucial role to play in helping get leaders and the wider workforce energized and focused on the right issues, and also in implementing Brexit strategy, where people issues will rank highly among the practical implications' (PwC, 2018).

I also was also interested in getting a view on Brexit from a talent acquisition perspective and spoke to Sam Allen, Managing Director at Sam Allen Associates and Orlando Martins, CEO and Founder of Oresa Executive Search regarding this.

Sam Allen notes that the implications of Brexit are starting to be felt in the recruitment industry. Specifically she observes that 'The UK can be seen as less attractive due to uncertainties; particularly the strength of the pound is not helpful to this.' In addition, 'Ex-pats see uncertainty of the future under Brexit as a deterrent to making a move to the UK.'

Orlando Martins comments:

With respect to Brexit and the likely impact on international talent in the UK, we believe that the ability of companies to attract CEO- and director-level talent will be largely unaffected due to the likely criteria for entering/remaining in the country. In contrast, however, we are concerned for all parts of the market that rely on highly skilled labour lower down the organization. In particular, luxury fashion, technology, hospitality and logistics are likely to suffer, with outsourcing and/or international relocations as potential outcomes. HR will need to be ready to evaluate complex people-led business cases and the impact on future strategy.

Social media

With social media now a part of everyday life it's perhaps not unexpected to see the growing trend of businesses promoting and selling their services and products through these channels. New functionality is being developed all the time, making it quicker and easier for consumers to see, click and buy in an instant.

We also see the growing prevalence of 'influencers' in this market in the form of bloggers or YouTubers who now play a key role for brands looking to establish themselves and gain credibility. Again, this is a particularly interesting trend for HR professionals to follow as we can learn a lot from how key influencers gain traction with their audience. It can be interesting to consider, for example, what makes a vlogger so compelling and how their techniques could be applied in the field of HR. For example, if we know that 90 per cent of our audience are more engaged through the medium of video and Facebook live, why are we still presenting them with lengthy hard-copy manuals and then wondering why our engagement scores continue to flatline?

Conclusion

It is important for all HR professionals to have a rudimentary understanding of which markets and channels the business they work in operates through. Through keeping up to date with market trends and changes they are then able to contribute and advise more effectively at a senior level. In addition, through being more aware of the political, social and economic factors that come into play in the global market they are then able to play a key role in strategy formation and business planning.

In terms of both markets and channels there is much that the HR professional can do on a strategic level to map across trends and experiences to the work being delivered by the HR function. This is a key factor in cultural congruency and establishing trust with the people working within the business.

Toolkit essentials: 5 steps to building an omnichannel HR function

1 Ensure a consistency of message across all communication media.

2 Develop a brand identity for HR that reflects the culture of the business and can be applied across all channels of communication.

3 Ensure that your team are all clear on the key messages and positioning of the function and that they back and believe the vision.

4 Ensure that the infrastructure of the HR function reflects the core positioning of the business in relation to customer experience. If you say you are a tech-forward business, ensure that your internal processes relating to employee experience also reflect this.

5 Always consider HR interventions in the context of a global market to ensure consistency and scalability.

Questions for reflection

Q. What markets does your business operate in?

Q. What channels does your business operate through?

Q. If you provide HR services or experiences across more than one channel, is the employee experience across all of the channels consistent?

Q. What materials or services does your business source from the global market?

Q. Who are the key influencers typically followed by the core customers of your business?

References

Financial Times Lexicon (2018) Global market definition, available at: http://lexicon.ft.com/Term?term=global-market [accessed 11 August 2018]

PwC (2018) Brexit: what are the implications for HR? Available at: www.pwc.co.uk/the-eu-referendum/brexit-what-are-implications-for-hr.html [accessed 11 August 2018]

Technology 14

Introduction

In this chapter our focus will be on developing awareness of key trends and factors relating to technology in the context of the business you operate in. This should be an essential consideration for any HR professional due to the business impact of technological change, and more so in the case of businesses who fall behind with this. Writing for *Forbes* in February 2017, Nick Morrison acknowledged rapid technological change as the biggest threat to global business. He quotes Frederick Fernandez, senior manager at consumer goods firm A.T. Kearney as saying, 'The consumer and retail industry will change more over the next 20 years than over the last 200 years. We have never lived in such exciting times' (Morrison, 2017).

How will this chapter shape my thinking?

- It will support you in evaluating your own businesses strategy with regard to technology.
- It will help you understand basic issues surrounding legacy systems and how these issues can derail and slow adoption of new technology.
- It will encourage you to consider how technological advancements might impact on the future shape of your workforce.
- It will support you in understanding how things get done with regards to tech change and project management through comparing Agile and Waterfall project management approaches.

Digital product

Digital product can be defined in a number of ways. From one perspective, digital product can be considered to be a product or a service that is purchased online and where no physical product exists; for example it could be a software download or an app. In addition, where Agile has been adopted within a business, McKinsey note that:

> Products can't be defined solely as commercial offerings. They may actually be combinations of offerings (for instance, a payroll service), or the customer experience (say, all the features and tasks that make up the online purchasing journey), or an IT system shared by multiple product teams (such as pricing software that generates quotes on demand)' (Comella-Dorda, Lohiya and Speksnijder, 2016).

It is possible to map this principle across to the HR function and therefore consider something such as the onboarding experience or a management skills development framework to be a 'product' in the same way. This is very useful to consider if Agile is also to be adopted across the wider business and in the HR function in addition to tech.

Legacy systems

Gartner define a legacy system as 'A system that may be based on outdated technologies, but is critical to day-to-day operations' (Gartner, 2018). With the rate of technological advancement, it becomes more and more likely that we will all encounter issues with legacy systems in the course of our careers and the impact of working in environments with extensive legacy systems should not be under-estimated. For example, if you operate in a progressive HR function and have aspirations to upgrade the employee experience within the business to reflect a more tech-forward approach you may encounter two issues. First, you may find that it's not possible to offer the type of experience you hope to provide through the existing legacy systems; they may just not be up to the job. Then you may find that you face something of a battle to get your project addressed in the backlog of tech work due to the prioritization of more immediately commercial projects. To an extent, the timescales for delivery and your ability to deliver are then taken out of your hands as a result of the issues arising from legacy systems.

There are potentially some other options to consider should you find yourself in this position and we'll look at those further on in this chapter in the section titled 'Start-ups and disruptors.'

Adoption

For many well-established businesses a key factor in implementing technological change at any level and particularly with regard to internal processes is ensuring that employees are on board with the change and are in a position where they are able to adopt the new systems with as little disruption as possible. HR clearly has a key role to play with regard to this and there are a number of factors to be considered. Perhaps one primary challenge is that experienced in a multi-generational workforce where digital natives are working alongside individuals who are still cautious and not as confident about embracing technology. However, in this particular scenario it is possible to leverage that difference as a strength and ensure mixed groups for launch and implementation activities so that those who are more confident in embracing the change are able to reassure and support others.

In the messaging to support tech adoption it is also essential to not only highlight 'why' the change is happening but also to draw out the benefits for the individual too. Where possible, test out the new process or system with groups of users over a period of time to get feedback and resolve some teething issues prior to launch. This point surrounding multi-generational workforces should not be underestimated because, as observed by Wes Gay in his article for *Forbes* in October 2017, 'For the first time in the modern age, we have five generations present in the workplace. From the Traditionalists born before 1945 all the way up until Gen Z' (Gay, 2017).

Talent disruption

The rate of technological change is also playing a significant role in the talent landscape and some very interesting scenarios are resulting from this, one being that traditionally non-tech businesses are now joining the race for tech talent. A great example of this is Jaguar Land Rover, who are committed to producing only electric or hybrid cars from 2020. As a result of this, the business has decided to open a tech hub in Manchester in recognition of the fact that the city is known as a centre of excellence for software engineers. They have announced plans to open this new software, IT and engineering centre to support their strategy to introduce connected technologies in future vehicles (Jaguar Land Rover, 2018). In the same way, a number of digital fashion businesses now also operate out of the Manchester area, such as Boohoo, Misguided and Pretty Little Thing to name a few. The point of consideration here is that we certainly find ourselves in interesting times when a car manufacturer and a fashion retailer end up competing for talent in the same space.

Start-ups and disruptors

Another interesting factor arising from the pace of tech advancement is the volume of start-up businesses emerging in this field and the disruptive impact they can now have in any organization. A great example of this in HR is in the area of HR systems and software. Where once this was a field monopolized by a few big names, now a significant number of smaller start-up businesses are stepping in and disrupting this through being able to respond more quickly and in a more agile way. In addition, they are also able to do this at a fraction of the cost as a result of their lower overheads.

One great showcase for start-ups and disruptors of tech in HR is the UNLEASH conference which currently runs three times a year, once in London, once in Amsterdam and once in the United States. The event has a dedicated start-up zone and the commitment to supporting them is clear, with a claim on their website that states that the 'UNLEASH Startup Ecosystem is the fastest-growing startup community in the world!' Further, the results of this focus and investment appear clear, with the following confirmation of results that have been achieved.

Since 2011, UNLEASH have showcased over 200 start-ups and many have gone on to achieve considerable success. Over US $1.5 billion has been raised in investments throughout this process with examples as follows:

- JobandTalent ($43m);
- Harver ($8.1m);
- Jobbatical ($3m);
- Impraise ($1.6m);
- Textio ($20m);
- Tandem ($2.5m);
- Klaxoon ($5m);
- Beamery ($5m);
- Praditus ($1.5m);
- CultureAmp ($36m);
- SmartRecruiters ($56m);
- Peakon ($6.5m);
- Glassdoor ($200m).

Project management: Agile and Waterfall

In Part One of this book we looked at how Agile can be applied in a non-tech environment for personal development, and in Part Four we will look at how it may impact on the future of the HR profession. However, for most businesses, the first implementation of Agile that we come across is in the IT or Tech team. In this world, Agile is not new and has strong roots in software development, but that's not to say that all Tech teams will be using it. In the course of your career it's likely that you will work in some organizations that have adopted

Agile and some that follow a more traditional 'Waterfall' approach. In order for you to effectively support this business area and contribute at a strategic level it is therefore important that you understand and have awareness of both.

According to *Techopedia*, Waterfall is 'A sequential software development process model that follows the following defined phases':

1 Conception

2 Initiation

3 Analysis

4 Design

5 Construction

6 Testing

7 Production/Implementation

8 Maintenance

(Techopedia.com, 2018a)

It's important to note that in this model it is advised that one step follows logically after the next and therefore that step should be completed before moving on to the next one. The prospect of returning to a previous step is viewed negatively.

In comparison, Agile is defined as 'A lightweight software engineering framework that promotes iterative development throughout the life-cycle of the project, close collaboration between the development team and business side, constant communication, and tightly knit teams' (Techopedia.com, 2018b).

In this scenario, progress is made through iterations and testing, meaning that it is highly likely that a previous step could be revisited as part of the development process.

Writing for *Forbes* in May 2017, Demian Entrekin, Chief Technology Officer at Bluescape, argues that Agile development has defeated Waterfall development to win the process battle in the software development world (Entrekin, 2017). He is, however, also quick to note that applying Agile alone is not going to be the primary solution for most businesses. His recommendation is to blend Agile with 'design thinking' in order to achieve the best results, noting:

While IT departments and software developers have been steadily shifting to agile development, management teams and business leaders have embraced the concept of design thinking. This is a form of creative process that aims to spark innovation and help organizations get their arms around the increasingly complex problems of today's marketplace' (Entrekin, 2017).

Conclusion

In order to effectively support an organization and to impact at a strategic level it is now more essential than ever for HR practitioners to have a good understanding of both the internal and external tech landscapes. From an internal perspective, having a good understanding of existing legacy systems within the business will ensure you are aware of how they will impact on proposed developments within the HR function and the wider business. In addition, understanding the backlog of work connected with legacy systems will support you in prioritizing and finding creative solutions to common HR challenges. In some cases it may be that you can find solutions through digital products created by start-ups and disruptors.

Through developing your understanding of how work gets done in the Tech team within your organization you will also be in a better position to support change and transformation in this area, which in turn supports business growth.

Toolkit essentials: 4 steps to increase your tech competence

1 Find a key contact in your Tech function and spend time with them within the function in order to develop your understanding of how things get done.

2 Keep up to speed with developments in HR technology, specifically with regard to start-ups and disruptors. Consider attending events such as UNLEASH, which are renowned for being showcases for this.

3 Consider how you utilize technology outside of work. Review ways in which technology is deployed to make your life easier and consider how similar concepts could be mapped across to employee experience.

4 Work with your Tech team to identify a tech-forward way to track projects for the HR function.

Questions for reflection

Q. What legacy systems exist within your business and is there a plan in place to update or replace them?

Q. Which legacy systems within your business are most likely to impact on your ability to deliver improved results though HR services and products?

Q. How could you channel and embrace multi-generational diversity to aid the uptake of technology in your organization?

Q. Who are your competitors when it comes to securing digital talent?

Q. What project management framework is used in the Tech function in your business?

References

Comella-Dorda, S, Lohiya, S and Speksnijder, G (2016) An operating model for company-wide agile development, *McKinsey & Company*, available at: www.mckinsey.com/business-functions/digital-mckinsey/our-insights/an-operating-model-for-company-wide-agile-development [accessed 12 August 2018]

Entrekin, D (2017) Agile is not enough, *Forbes*, available at: www.forbes.com/sites/forbestechcouncil/2017/05/19/agile-is-not-enough/#332811094bfb [accessed 14 August 2018]

Gartner (2018) Legacy application or system, *Gartner IT Glossary*, available at: www.gartner.com/it-glossary/legacy-application-or-system [accessed 12 August 2018]

Gay, W (2017) Why a multigenerational workforce is a competitive advantage, *Forbes*, available at: www.forbes.com/sites/ wesgay/2017/10/20/multigeneration-workforce/#744b44f44bfd [accessed 12 August 2018]

Jaguar Land Rover (2018) Jaguar Land Rover opens Manchester hub developing next generation of connected cars, available at: https://media.jaguarlandrover.com/news/2018/06/jaguar-land-rover-opens-manchester-hub-developing-next-generation-connected-cars [accessed 12 August 2018]

Morrison, N (2017) Rapid technological change is the biggest threat to global business, Forbes, available at: www.forbes.com/sites/ nickmorrison/2017/02/09/donald-trump-is-not-the-biggest-threat-to-global-business/#701f74891b73 [accessed 12 August 2018]

Techopedia.com (2018a) What is Waterfall model? Available at: www. techopedia.com/definition/14025/waterfall-model [accessed 14 August 2018]

Techopedia.com (2018b) What is Agile software development? Available at: www.techopedia.com/definition/13564/agile-software-development [accessed 14 August 2018]

Unleash (2018) The Unleashed startup connection, available at: www.unleashgroup.io/startup?utm_source=google&utm_ medium=search&utm_campaign=ams2018&utm_term=brand&utm_ content=version_2-6C&gclid=CjwKCAjw-8nbBRBnEiwAqWt1zV-L4QLI0lyxd4Qt8YCTBvFy3mBhKp0VTHGYJ82JjOoz_y03JMsp7z-RoC9pYQAvD_BwE [Accessed 14 August 2018]

Purpose and values

Introduction

In this chapter we will look at the concept of 'purpose' and explore what this means for the organization you work in. We'll consider how to develop and communicate an authentic purpose and look at how this connects with the real values of the business. The dictionary defines the purpose of something as 'the reason for which it is made or done'. In addition, it says, 'Purpose is the feeling of having a definite aim and of being determined to achieve it.' It is perhaps this definition that is key to bringing energy and vitality to 'purpose' in an organizational context in order to ensure that employees within the business feel a connection with it and a shared sense of determination can then be cultivated.

How will this chapter shape my thinking?

- It will support you in reviewing your current organizational purpose and assess if it is one that facilitates a meaningful connection with employees.
- It will help you connect purpose and values in a cohesive way that reflects your brand identity.
- It will help you map across 'purpose' to matters of corporate social responsibility, ensuring an authentic connection and congruency.

Authenticity

All too often it can be the case that organizations create some form of purpose statement that ends up being little more than a printed slogan on a mouse mat. Typically, the root cause of this is that the words just don't resonate as reality or even as a possibility for the employees within the business. In scenarios like this, the outcome typically becomes that at best the purpose statement is ignored, and at worst it becomes a factor that impacts on trust within the business and damages the employee/employer relationship. For example, if the purpose statement suggests that the employer is an advocate for ethical trade but it's known within the business that this is not always the case, the statement does nothing to motivate or inspire employees and actually exists in a way that damages credibility. It may well be that the business has created the purpose in such a way as to be aspirational but more often than not the gap between the reality and aspiration can be too great to bridge.

Another potential pitfall here is where the 'purpose' is defined in isolation by the executive team or by one individual. In order to achieve real authenticity with the words it is essential to cultivate ideas from a number of areas within the business and from employees at all levels. This holistic view then enables the senior team to effectively blend the vision and the aspiration with the reality of life in the business and create a statement with a shared meaning that resonates and motivates people effectively.

Values

Many of the above principles that relate to authenticity also apply to the creation of values within an organization. If a purpose statement serves to unite people with a shared passion and motivate them to achieve, values become the 'way things get done' and can almost be considered as the personality traits of the business. In creating or articulating values, again a cross-section of employees should be involved in the process in order to maintain authenticity and also to support buy-in when the values are communicated and launched. Please refer to the 'Toolkit essentials' section in this chapter for additional information on how to achieve this.

Another key factor here is to ensure that managers and leaders within the business identify with and respect the values as they will need to role model them and inspire their teams to embrace them. If managers and leaders openly flout the values and act in a way that contradicts them the values will instantly be rejected by employees and discredited.

In order for values to be really effective they need to be relevant to the organization and to feel relevant and inspiring for employees. A good test for this would be that if you took the company name off them would they still be identifiable as relating to your business. If not, it's likely that they are too generic, and employees are less likely to connect with them as a result of this.

Communication

Once the purpose and values have been agreed it is essential to communicate them effectively and ensure a consistency of message across the whole organization. They should be intrinsically linked to business processes and reinforced in a way that reflects the culture of the business. In addition, they also need to be communicated effectively to prospective employees as part of the resourcing process. If written and communicated effectively, values play a key role in creating and preserving the culture of the business and the value of this should not be underestimated. An example of this could be where a brand is launching in a new territory and is aspiring to attract the best talent to work for the business in that location. This can be incredibly challenging if people are not aware of the brand and don't have the connection with it that people in the brand's home country do. In this scenario, well-presented brand values and purpose help forge a connection with potential employees and help build the vision for why the business exists and what individuals will be a part of if they come onboard. The more effective the channels of communication are, the deeper the level of connection with individuals will be.

CSR

When considering the purpose of an organization, it's also useful to map this across to matters of corporate social responsibility (CSR), which can be defined as 'The incorporation of ethical elements, such as the public interest and environmental concern, into the planning of business strategy' (Collinsdictionary.com, 2018b). The truth is that CSR comes in many different forms across different organizations, with some fully embracing it and others not; it can encompass activities that support the local community right through to supporting or leading initiatives on a national and international level. Where a business can link its purpose with CSR activities the benefits of the activity are magnified, both internally and externally. This helps to further rally employees behind achieving the purpose through inspiring them in creative ways and also, from an external perspective, helps to build trust and credibility with consumers. An example of this could be in an organization that has a purpose linked to improving quality of life through access to technology. If they also engaged in CSR activity such as supporting tech start-ups in the relevant area through an incubator programme they really would be perceived as living their purpose.

Writing for *Forbes* in August 2018, Jim Ludema and Amber Johnson take this connection with CSR a step further, drawing out six CSR strategies that are good for business. Specifically they highlight:

1 aligning CSR to business strategy;

2 build engagement at all levels, starting at the top;

3 look for opportunities linked to talent acquisition;

4 achieving results faster through forging partnerships;

5 finding new drivers of innovation;

6 integrating design thinking approaches.

(Ludema and Johnson, 2018)

From this we can determine that CSR can be leveraged for commercial advantage and also becomes a key consideration connecting internal and external perceptions of purpose and values.

Conclusion

All organizations have a purpose, as without one they simply wouldn't exist. It can, however, sometimes be a challenge to effectively articulate this purpose in a way that engages and motivates people. The key tactic here is to ensure that employees can get involved in creating the purpose and that it is brought to life for them in a way that resonates both with the reality and the aspiration of the organization. Purpose is further strengthened through values that articulate how things get done and then further authenticity is achieved via linking purpose and values externally, potentially through the channel of CSR.

Toolkit essentials: 5 steps to create brand values

1 Obtain the view of the senior team, framing the question of 'If this brand was a person, what personality traits would they have?'

2 Set up focus groups with a cross-section of employees at all levels to cultivate their feedback and ideas.

3 Involve the wider business and obtain feedback and ideas through conducting an anonymous survey.

4 Collate the information gathered from all sources and present to a working party with a cross representation of employees from different business sectors and at different levels.

5 Through the working party compile a list of approx. 5 short values statements from the feedback which most resonate with the business.

Questions for reflection

Q. What is the 'purpose' of the business you work in? Why does it exist?

Q. Do your brand values act as enablers to the purpose?

Q. If your organization was a person, what personality traits would it have? Do your values reflect this or is there a disconnect between aspiration and reality?

Q. How are your brand values and purpose communicated to employees?

Q. Who has responsibility for CSR in your business and what CSR activities are currently in place that support the brand purpose and values?

References

Collinsdictionary.com (2018a) Purpose definition and meaning, available at: www.collinsdictionary.com/dictionary/english/purpose [accessed 15 August 2018]

Collinsdictionary.com (2018) Corporate social responsibility definition and meaning, available at: www.collinsdictionary.com/dictionary/english/corporate-social-responsibility [accessed 15 August 2018]

Ludema, J and Johnson, A (2018) Six CSR strategies that are good for business, *Forbes*, available at: www.forbes.com/sites/amberjohnson-jimludema/2018/08/15/six-csr-strategies-that-are-good-for-business/#4d9d93ed50a8 [accessed 16 August 2018]

PART THREE
Know your industry

Competition   16

Introduction

In this chapter we begin our focus on looking at the concept of 'knowing your industry' and in particular the concept of 'competition', investigating what it means for your business and how it applies at industry level. The *Business Dictionary* defines competition as 'Rivalry in which every seller tries to get what other sellers are seeking at the same time: sales, profit, and market share by offering the best practicable combination of price, quality, and service. Where the market information flows freely, competition plays a regulatory function in balancing demand and supply' (BusinessDictionary.com, 2018).

How will this chapter shape my thinking?

- It will help you to effectively identify both the obvious and not-so-obvious competitors within the industry you work in.
- It will support you in identifying the positive benefits of competition.
- It will encourage you to identify ways in which you can support your organization in achieving competitive advantage.

Identification of competitors

When you consider the industry that your business operates in, competitors will typically fall into two categories. There will be the ones that are immediately obvious because they either provide similar services or sell similar products to the same pool of customers that you do. Then there will be competitors that fall outside of this remit who are not so obvious but who also compete for the disposable income of the customers your business is targeting. There will be established competitors and also emerging competitors whose businesses are enabled in disruptive ways through technology.

One example here is the industry of fashion retail, which we will look at in Figure 16.1.

We start from the position of looking at bricks-and-mortar stores and in this scenario it's clear to see that a number of retailers operate in that format; there are several brands that are in competition with each other, with customers browsing between the different physical locations. Then, expanding that into e-commerce, we see that additional competitors are added in a fairly obvious way in that there are other fashion retailers who compete for the same customers but whose business exists only online. It could be argued that they have some competitive advantage here due to the lower overheads achieved through not investing in physical stores. So, at a surface level we can identify direct competitors providing similar products in the fashion retail industry, some operating with the same business model and some operating through a purely digital business model.

Figure 16.1   Example competition map for fashion retail

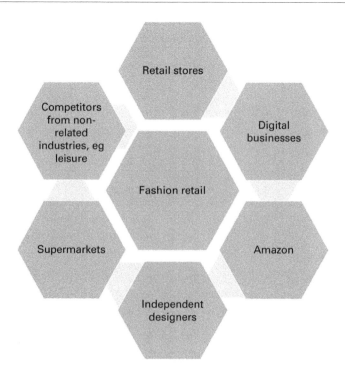

Next we move on to investigate the not-so-obvious competitors and in this case we look at other retailers who operate outside of pure 'fashion' retail. For some fashion brands, particularly the price players, competition in this form can also come from supermarkets who have significantly expanded their fashion offering in recent years.

It's also important to look at the impact of Amazon, who have also disrupted a number of industries through their business model. Their scale and presence can't be ignored and as they also grow their fashion ranges in relation to the 'fashion retail' industry example we can see how they are quickly becoming a competitor that needs to be considered. Next, on a smaller scale it's also important to note in this industry the smaller start-up brands and designers who have now set up tech-enabled businesses and who now compete well against larger brands through their social media presence.

Lastly, we consider competition from non-related industries who also compete with us for the customer's disposable income. For example, it's realistic to assume that in some scenarios a customer may choose to invest in a leisure activity over deciding to spend money that month on an additional piece of clothing.

Activity 6

Create your own competitor map for your industry and identify both the obvious and not-so-obvious competitors to the business you operate in.

Benefits of competition

It's important to note that in most cases competition should be viewed as a positive thing; it's true that it doesn't always bring out the best in people but in a corporate environment it can have significant advantages. In an article that appeared in *Inc* magazine, James Park, co-founder of Fitbit, comments on the fact that his big competitors in Nike and Jawbone have helped his business by 'Lending it an air of credibility and generating some buzz in the press.' He notes that 'More players in the market implies that wearable tech is a mainstream activity and that consumers should be comfortable adopting it'. He goes on to add, 'You need some critical mass to legitimize what you're doing' (Krasny, 2018).

In addition to building credibility in the market, there are numerous benefits that arise through healthy competition as it constantly pushes an organization to be better and to improve customer service. This alone can become a determining factor in driving additional revenue through providing an exceptional customer experience that competitors find it hard to replicate.

Another significant benefit of competition that can be used for tactical advantage is in the case of an organization that is comfortable in operating as a 'fast follower' and not necessarily pushing to be leading the way with regards to innovation. The benefit of being a 'fast follower' in a competitive market is that you can observe and learn from the mistakes of other businesses. It can be a risky strategy though, so any business adopting it needs to be set up to act fast on the lessons learned and be ready to implement and apply them in a commercial way so as not to be left behind.

Supporting competitive advantage

With regards to making a strategic contribution through HR, competitive advantage should be an integral area to focus on. It is essential that you understand how your business currently achieves competitive advantage and ensure that these activities are adequately supported. It could be argued that for any business, people are the primary source of advantage here as they create the products and services that are sold to generate revenue. Therefore, from this it's clear to see how important the involvement of HR becomes within the constructs of 'competition'.

Writing for the *Harvard Business Review* in 2008, Rita Gunther McGrath looks further at how to connect HR with competitive advantage and observed a particular link with enabling innovation. She notes, 'A strategically minded HR department can craft jobs, create networks among people, and provide the training that helps every person in the organization become part of its innovation engine' (Gunther McGrath, 2008). Thus HR becomes a key component in creating competitive advantage.

In addition, another key factor to consider here is the role HR professionals play with regard to securing and retaining talent for the organization. Writing for her blog *The HR Bartender* in 2017, Sharlyn Lauby observes three steps to enable recruitment as a source of competitive advantage:

1 properly staff your talent acquisition team;
2 train the talent acquisition team;
3 give recruiters the tools to do the job.

(Lauby, 2017)

Although basic, these three steps have a significant impact on the ability of any talent acquisition team to perform and should not be overlooked in consideration of their effect on competitive advantage.

Conclusion

To ensure the success of the business you work in and to enable you to make an impact at a commercial level it is imperative for all HR professionals to have a firm grasp on competitor activity and sources of competitive advantage within the organizations they operate in. This should be considered first through mapping out known competitors and also considering emerging ones. HR professionals can play a significant role in leveraging the positive benefits of competition, specifically with regard to fostering a culture and environment that supports innovation. In addition, HR plays a key role here through talent acquisition and retention as it is clear that people form the biggest source of competitive advantage with a mix of unique skills that cannot easily be replicated. This is particularly so in the case of key employees who hold significant tacit knowledge or influence within an organization. If HR professionals are not aware of the key players and skills that drive competitive advantage for the business their credibility will be affected and their ability to truly operate from a strategic and commercial position will be compromised.

Toolkit essentials: 5 steps to help you build awareness of competitor activity

1 Ensure you keep up to date with industry news through reading the trade press for your industry.

2 Maintain awareness of emerging competitors from outside of your industry through identifying sources of business news, eg *Forbes*, *Inc.*, *Financial Times*.

3 Research tech start-ups and incubator programmes to get an idea of emerging trends and developments.

4 Engage with a contact in your Marketing function and establish how market share is measured and tracked for your business.

5 Attend relevant trade and industry events for the purpose of networking and collating information that helps you further understand competitor activity.

Questions for reflection

Q. What action can you take this week in order to make your talent acquisition strategy more competitive?

Q. How does corporate competition positively benefit your organization?

Q. How can you actively support innovation within your business?

References

BusinessDictionary.com (2018) What is competition? Definition and meaning, available at: http://www.businessdictionary.com/definition/competition.html [accessed 16 August 2018]

Gunther McGrath, R (2008) Connecting HR with competitive advantage, *Harvard Business Review*, available at: https://hbr.org/2008/06/connecting-hr-with-competitive [accessed 16 August 2018]

Krasny, J (2018) Why competition may be the best thing for your business, *Inc.*, available at: www.inc.com/magazine/201311/jill-krasny/more-competition-is-better-for-start-ups.html [accessed 16 August 2018]

Lauby, S (2017) 3 steps to make recruiting your competitive advantage, *HR Bartender*. available at: www.hrbartender.com/2017/recruiting/recruiting-competitive-advantage/ [accessed 16 August 2018]

Business environment

17

Introduction

In this chapter we will look at the business environment and draw out key factors that it is essential for all HR professionals to be aware of in order to operate at a strategic level. According to the *Business Dictionary*, 'business environment' can be defined as 'The combination of internal and external factors that influence a company's operating situation. The business environment can include factors such as: clients and suppliers; its competition and owners; improvements in technology; laws and government activities; and market, social and economic trends' (BusinessDictionary.com, 2018). This is an important topic for individuals working within HR who aspire to contribute strategically beyond the remit of their own function as this knowledge supports in early identification of trends and issues which may affect the overall commercial performance of the organization and through this will empower you to be proactive in delivering solutions.

How will this chapter shape my thinking?

- It will help you identify where you can access information relating to the environment that your business operates in.
- It will encourage you to use this knowledge as a core part of your strategic planning for the HR function.
- It will help you broaden your frames of reference in relation to how the business operates.
- It will help you evaluate your contribution to the success of the business in line with external environmental factors.

Building awareness

In order to develop your awareness of the external environment it's important to consistently invest time in keeping your knowledge up to date. This can be done in a number of ways, and reading the trade press for your industry can be a good place to start. It is also helpful to read related press to broaden awareness; for example, you may choose to read a publication on supply chain management if your business has a sizeable supply chain operation. In addition, digital resources are a quick and easy way to get a feel for emerging trends relating to business environment; *Bloomberg Businessweek*, *Forbes* and *Harvard Business Review* are all good sources of data.

Another suggestion here to support you in building awareness of relevant environmental developments is to ensure you are also talking to your colleagues and key stakeholders within the business about it, particularly with regard to emerging technology. An example here could be that you invest time in understanding where the Tech team get their inspiration and external knowledge from. How are they keeping up to date with external environmental factors etc. In addition, if you have a 'new business' or 'business development' function within your organization, this team should be in a good position to advise you on how they map the external landscape and track trends to support business growth.

Connecting your strategy

After building your awareness of the external business environment and ensuring that you keep up to speed with changes and developments you then need to integrate this knowledge with your HR strategy. Through doing this you then start to make the transition from just getting things done to getting the *right* things done at the right time. Writing for *SHRM* in 2017, Eric Friedman notes that there are four external environmental factors that particularly impact on HR and which should definitely appear in some context within your strategy. Specifically, these are government regulations, economic conditions, technological advancements and workforce demographics (Friedman, 2017). All of these factors have an impact on your ability to recruit and retain great people and to establish processes which then enable those people to deliver great work within the organization.

Another important thing to consider here is the essential need to bring external information into your strategic planning process. Writing for *Forbes* in 2017, Bernard Marr references Jorn Lyseggen, author of *Outside Insight: Navigating a world drowning in data*. He quotes Lyseggen in relation to the issues arising from only adopting a review of internal data and statistics as saying, 'It's only about you. It's lagging performance indicators – you are seeing the shadows of opportunities that you had in the past.' Marr goes on to add:

> Making the switch to a focus on external data means it's no longer only about you. By monitoring and analysing the disparate data sources available thanks to our always-online and connected world, it's possible for an organization to build an awareness of the environment around them (Marr, 2017).

It is suggested that this point around internal data providing only shadows of past opportunities further highlights the absolute requirement for HR professionals to ensure they are consistently bringing new thinking and insight to the business and in particular ensuring that they integrate this into their strategic planning.

PESTEL analysis

A key tool to deploy in order to strengthen your skills in terms of mapping the external environment and then utilizing the data effectively is a PESTLE analysis. The CIPD describe this as 'A framework to analyse the key factors influencing an organization from the outside. HR practitioners and senior managers can use the results of this analysis to guide strategic decision making' (CIPD, 2017). The elements to this analysis are as follows:

- **Political.** Factors in this category relate to ways in which a government may intervene and impact on an economy. This could be through policy, legislation and trade restrictions.

- **Economic.** In this category factors can have a significant impact on the overall profitability of a business, for example interest rates, inflation, exchange rates, economic growth and disposable income for consumers.

- **Sociological.** In this section, factors relating to shared social beliefs and attitudes amongst a population are included. This could be linked to health and wellbeing considerations, population growth, immigration, age demographics and attitudes towards careers and lifestyle.

- **Technological.** Without doubt the fastest area of change, this section includes factors relating to how technology is utilized by organizations and consumers, specifically in relation to development and distribution of new products and services. Other considerations here link to new channels of communication and how technology is deployed as an enabler of lifestyle change.

- **Environmental.** In this section of the analysis, now standard environmental factors should be considered, eg carbon footprint, sustainable and fair trade requirements, and pollution targets; in this section we also now bring in issues connected with ethical trade.

- **Legal.** Factors here range from consumer rights and laws to data protection, health and safety, and product safety. Factors concerning operating and licensing for businesses are also considered.

Activity 7

Complete a PESTEL analysis for the organization you work in and when completed test your findings with two colleagues both working in different departments within the business.

Conclusion

A business that only looks inwards is sure to fail and by that rationale an HR function that only looks inwards is also going to

fail in any attempts to make a meaningful impact. HR professionals must ensure that they remain relevant and aware of external
factors in the wider business environment in order to incorporate
trends and developments into their HR strategy. Through building
on existing relationships with key contacts in the organization,
HR can amplify their results and reputation through building
partnerships that support the organization beyond the remit of
traditional HR, for example through collaborations with business development. It can often be the case that in the day-to-day
running of the HR operation it can be easy to forget how effective deployment of analysis models can be; a regular review of the
business through the PESTEL model can establish a framework
and process through which external issues can be picked up easily
and reviewed.

Toolkit essentials: 5 steps to help you incorporate factors impacting on the external business environment into your work

1 Attend a mix of events and meet-ups, some connected specifically to the industry you work in, some purely aimed at tech disruptors, and some where the focus is general business development.

2 Establish who the key influencers are in the industry you operate in and follow their work both through social media and by reading new publications.

3 Work with a mentor who can support you in navigating matters concerning the external business environment.

4 Find a way that works for you to keep yourself updated, either through reading physical publications, subscribing to podcasts, watching the news or subscribing to business updates.

5 Establish ways to share the information you collate in a way that supports other individuals within your organization and the organization as a whole.

Questions for reflection

Q. Does your current HR strategy reflect developments in the wider business environment?

Q. Who is responsible for new business development in the organization you work in? In what ways can you collaborate with them?

Q. What are your sources of external information with regard to business environment and how do you ensure you remain up to speed with developments?

References

BusinessDictionary.com (2018) Business environment, available at: www.businessdictionary.com/definition/business-environment.html [accessed 20 August 2018]

CIPD (2017) PESTLE analysis factsheets, available at: www.cipd.co.uk/ knowledge/strategy/organisational-development/pestle-analysis-factsheet [accessed 20 August 2018]

Friedman, E (2017) 4 external factors that affect human resource management, *SHRM,* available at: https://blog.shrm.org/blog/ 4-external-factors-that-affect-human-resource-management [accessed 20 August 2018]

Marr, B (2017) Outside insight: why external data is the fuel of tomorrow's business success, *Forbes*, available at: www.forbes.com/ sites/bernardmarr/2017/11/15/outside-insight-why-external-data-is-the-fuel-of-tomorrows-business-success/#405224b85e1d [accessed 20 August 2018]

Rules and regulations 18

Introduction

In this chapter our focus will be on business rules and regulations. We will explore some key areas linked to this that are specifically relevant to HR professionals and also establish how we can broaden our strategic contribution through building awareness of general business rules and regulations. Every organization that exists is bound by the constraints and enablers of regulation in some form and a key factor in being able to operate at a senior level and extend your contribution beyond the remit of HR is to understand this. Further information on the various rules and regulations beyond this overview and introduction can and should be sourced directly as relevant to your specific organization and industry.

How will this chapter shape my thinking?

- It will help you to understand the risks associated with intellectual property and consider what steps you can take to mitigate them.

- It will help you identify opportunities arising from new legislation, eg GDPR.

- It will encourage you to consider competition law and how this applies to your business.

- It will demonstrate how you can take key principles from consumer rights law and utilize them to improve the quality and perception of the HR products and services you and your team deliver.

GDPR

In May 2018, Bernard Marr considered the impact of GDPR specifically in relation to HR teams in an article that appeared in *Forbes*. Marr noted that 'GDPR represents a complete overhaul of the legal requirements that must be met by any company handling EU citizens' personal data'. Marr highlighted the key consideration for HR as being the issue of consent connected with purpose, noting that 'GDPR states that companies can only use personal data for the *express purpose* for which it was given. For HR teams, this means employees must explicitly opt in to allow their employer to use their personal data, and they must be made fully aware of how that data will be used' (Marr, 2018).

Looking at the impact on the wider business it's important to establish the opportunities that this new legislation brings. Speaking at the UNLEASH conference in 2018, Ardi Kolah drew out the key principles of this, noting that 'The genesis behind the regulation was lowering barriers to entry and creating more choice for consumers. On that basis, GDPR should be seen as an opportunity. Yes, we have to keep security and protection in mind, but we also need to remember that a lot of this relates to commercial competition' (Beaven, 2018).

It's true that GDPR does bring more work but it should be acknowledged that this is a positive thing in relation to the outcomes it brings, as it ultimately ensures a level of transparency that builds trust with both consumers and employees. It provides an opportunity to improve and to be better; at a basic level, compliance can be achieved in three simple steps:

1 Establish the risks: look at where data is held and what it is used for.

2 Take steps to mitigate the risks: take action on what you have uncovered to improve systems, processes and awareness.

3 Record what you've done: maintain records of any training and actions taken so that you have robust data to demonstrate your actions should the need arise.

To further explore practical implications for HR I also interviewed Keith Budden, Managing Director, GDPR Training Course (www.gdprtrainingcourse.co.uk) who shared the following advice.

GDPR and HR: Insights from Keith Budden

GDPR is looked upon by many as an obligation (which it is), but done correctly GDPR also represents a great business opportunity. Your current employees' morale can be boosted by knowing that you are taking the security of their data seriously and that the transparency afforded by the new regulations means that they can (if they wish) be aware of what is being recorded about them. But it is also a big recruitment message too – if you show potential employees early in the recruitment process that you have fully embraced GDPR, they will feel confident they are moving into a safe environment where their privacy will be protected. But do remember that if you introduce any new employee processes, you should conduct a Data Privacy Impact Assessment to ensure that you are not introducing new risks to the integrity of your employee data.

GDPR impacts several different aspects of HR:

- **Recruitment**. An obvious part of the recruitment process is communicating with applicants, so clearly by completing an application form and/or sending you their CV, an applicant is consenting to you contacting them – but only about employment. It's not a reason for adding them to your marketing database (even if you are a recruitment agency, they are giving consent for one role, and if you want wider consent for marketing etc you should explicitly ask for it).

  The other issue is what you do with the CVs/application details of unsuccessful applicants. Traditionally many of us would have kept the details of those who applied unsuccessfully for the current role but who may still be good candidates for future roles so we had easy access to them. You can still retain those details but you must get the applicants' explicit consent. You should also have a clear policy on retention, ie you keep their details for six months, and have a regular purge to ensure that retention policy is being observed.

- **DBS checks**. There are obviously some appointments where a DBS check is a very necessary part of the recruitment process; however, as GDPR places implications on proving the necessity of holding any item of information, best practice is that a DBS check is not requested until, at the earliest, there is a tightly defined shortlist of candidates, and ideally not until you are in a position to make a job offer.

- **Employee privacy policy**. Every member of staff should be given two copies of your privacy policy. The employee should sign and date one copy of the policy which you should retain on the employee's HR record. Please note that it is no longer acceptable to have your staff privacy policy covered in a couple of paragraphs of your Contract of Employment; it must be a physically separate document. Employees must be free to either sign or not sign your staff privacy policy. In itself, not signing the policy is not a reason to bring disciplinary action against the employee. Our experience has been that in practice, any employee reluctant to sign can normally be persuaded to do so if given a chance to air their concerns and you (or your GDPR data protection officer) can provide sufficient reassurance.

- **Internal CCTV**. If you use CCTV internally within your premises, details of this must be included in your staff privacy policy, including how a member of staff can request to view any CCTV in which they appear. You need to think carefully about your reasons for using CCTV in the workplace, whether for security or employee health and safety. A tribunal recently found that using CCTV in the corridor used to access the staff toilets (not in the toilets themselves) was an unwarranted invasion of privacy for the employees concerned.

- **Employees and the right to be forgotten**. The GDPR right to data deletion/the cessation of processing of data about an individual, commonly known as 'The Right to be Forgotten', does not apply to either current or ex-employees (although for ex-employees check the section below).

- **After someone leaves your employment**. An employee leaving means that you need to consider the necessity of what information about that employee you wish to retain. While there is a legitimate argument for retaining core employee details, plus any reviews/disciplinary action etc, there is no legitimate argument for retaining details of the employee's family, their next of kin, or any medications they were taking regularly. All such information should be removed from their employee records, or at least redacted.

- **An employee subject to disciplinary action**. Where an employee is subject to disciplinary action, that employee now has a right to see all records (both computerized and on paper) that you hold on them, together with any mobile phone text messages relating to them. It is therefore sensible, where an employee's performance is being assessed, to encourage your team to do that either face to face, or by telephone voice call, rather than via an SMS conversation.

Intellectual property

The rules and regulations surrounding intellectual property (IP) are of particular importance as they protect the competitive advantage that results from the work or talent of individuals within a business. *All About Law* notes that 'Intellectual property law (commonly known as IP) governs the ownership and accessibility of ideas and inventions on tangible and intangible concepts. In an extremely competitive world, IP is an integral part of business' (*All About Law*, 2018).

From a strategic HR perspective there are two main factors to be aware of here. First, and perhaps the most obvious place to start, is that it is important to ensure that the IP of the business is protected appropriately in the form of employment contracts. Essentially, this ensures that should any employee be lured away from the business by a competitor or leave in order to set up their own competing business, appropriate safeguards are in place to limit their ability to take designs, inventions and IP with them.

Then there is a secondary factor to consider of ensuring that employees within the business are aware of IP law in order to protect the business from litigation should any employee consciously or unconsciously 'copy' the work of another individual or competitor. This is of particular concern in the fashion industry but also extends beyond that. An example of how this materializes in practice can be referenced through a case reported in 2010 where fashion retailer AllSaints instigated legal action against River Island for intellectual property infringement, claiming that a number of designs had been copied (Shields, 2010). In addition, in the year prior to that another fashion retailer 'Superdry' brought a similar case against Primark and received a settlement from them in relation to the copy of a leather jacket. It is therefore essential to ensure appropriate training is provided for individuals who are involved in creating, designing and inventing products and services in order that they are aware of legislation in this area and through that limit risk to the business.

Consumer rights

For any business that sells products or services, consumer law and regulation will apply. As noted by *Which?* (2018):

> The Consumer Rights Act 2015 became law on 1 October 2015, replacing three major pieces of consumer legislation – the Sale of Goods Act, Unfair Terms in Consumer Contracts Regulations, and the Supply of Goods and Services Act. It was introduced to simplify, strengthen and modernize the law, giving clearer shopping rights.

Essentially this legislation provides that physical and digital goods and services must meet the following criteria. They must be:

- of satisfactory quality;
- fit for the purpose indicated;
- as described physically or digitally.

This legislation is important to consider in the context of your role, particularly at a more senior level, as it prompts you to evaluate the quality and ethical positioning of the products and services provided by the organization you work for. It could be suggested that in order for you to deliver your best work you should ensure you are in a position where you feel you can fully endorse those products and services.

In addition, it is also possible to relate the principles of this legislation across to the products and services delivered by the HR function within the business. It can be an interesting activity to test a product or service release with the three factors identified here, effectively positioning the employees within the business as end users or consumers of the work your function has created.

Activity 8

Select one product or service that has been released to the business by the HR team in the last 12 months. Identify a key stakeholder who would have been identified as a customer or 'user' of this product or service. Connect with that stakeholder and ask them the following;

1 Was the end product/service of satisfactory quality for them? If not, what could have been improved?

2 Was it fit for purpose? Did it do the job they needed it to and that you expected it to?

3 Was it as described? Did they get what they thought they were going to get? Did your launch and pre-launch communication ensure there were no surprises or disappointments when the product or service was launched?

Competition law

According to the Financial Conduct Authority (FCA, 2018) competition law forbids:

- cartels and other potentially anti-competitive agreements, and
- abuse of a dominant position.

Investigating this legislation will support you in understanding wider issues surrounding your industry, business environment and competitor activity. It will also encourage you to investigate your own company's pricing strategy further and consider the organization's position in the market.

In terms of the first point regarding cartels and anti-competitive agreements, the FCA notes that 'Examples of cartels include agreements to fix prices or share markets. Examples of other potentially anti-competitive agreements include a distributor agreeing with its supplier not to sell below a particular price' (FCA, 2018).

It is important to note that abuse of a dominant position can be categorized as a position where one business, essentially a dominant one in a specific market, makes a decision to price their goods or services so low that they don't even cover the costs incurred in delivery or sale of that product or service. This tactic is typically deployed with the aim of driving competitor organizations out of business, leaving the original organization in a position where they can then increase their costs again without fear of competition and certainly to the detriment of the consumer.

Conclusion

The volume of legislation impacting on the operating practices of organizations is vast and beyond the scope of this text to cover in detail here. However, there are some key rules and regulations that are important to draw out specifically in relation to enabling strategic contribution from HR professionals operating at a senior level. Although not always perceived as being an immediately engaging area of HR practice there are opportunities here that can be applied in creative ways in order to enhance the HR function and overall strategic contribution of individuals working within it.

Toolkit essentials: 4 additional key areas of legislation to ensure you are familiar with in order to enhance your strategic contribution

1 Employment law in all territories in which your organization operates.

2 Health and safety legislation.

3 EU Withdrawal Bill

4 Bribery and corruption.

References

All About Law (2018) Intellectual property law, available at: www.allaboutlaw.co.uk/stage/areas-of-law/intellectual-property-law [accessed 21 August 2018]

Beaven, K (2018) Countdown to GDPR: Are you ready? *Unleashed*, available at: www.unleashgroup.io/news/countdown-to-gdpr-are-you-ready [accessed 21 August 2018]

FCA (2018) Competition law, available at: www.fca.org.uk/about/promoting-competition/powers [accessed 21 August 2018]

Marr, B (2018) What does GDPR really mean for HR teams? *Forbes*, available at: www.forbes.com/sites/bernardmarr/2018/04/27/what-does-gdpr-really-mean-for-hr-teams/#23df233a30e0 [accessed 21 August 2018]

Shields, R (2010) Inspired, or fashion theft? *Independent*, available at: www.independent.co.uk/life-style/fashion/news/inspired-or-fashion-theft-1863267.html [accessed 21 August 2018]

Which? (2018) Consumer Rights Act 2015, *Which? Consumer Rights*, available at: www.which.co.uk/consumer-rights/regulation/consumer-rights-act [accessed 21 August 2018]

Trends and forecasting 19

Introduction

Writing for *Inc.* magazine in 2018, Jeffrey Phillips, senior consultant at RTI Innovation Advisors noted that 'The best innovations don't start with ideas, regardless of what you think or have been told. They start with noticing evolving and emerging trends, and understanding customer needs' (Phillips, 2018). In this chapter we look at the topic of trends and forecasting in order to identify what role this plays in the industry in which our organization operates. We then map this across to its importance in relation to the commercial success of our business and then consider what thinking and processes can be applied to Human Resources.

> ### How will this chapter shape my thinking?
>
> - It will enhance your awareness of industry trends and how to access data relating to this.
> - It will encourage you to incorporate elements of trend forecasting in your strategic planning processes.
> - It will support you in developing your awareness of how business development decisions are made in the organization you work in.
> - It will encourage you to consider the limitations of trend forecasting in the context of strategic planning.

Emerging trends

There are a vast number of factors when considering emerging trends that will impact on the organization you work in, and depending on the nature of your business a vast number of places from which to start an analysis. As a starting point, some sources of information relating to external trends are:

- trade conferences;
- trade press;
- start-up incubators;
- social media;
- mainstream media;
- agencies and businesses supplying trend data and insights.

For most businesses the best place to start is to review trends concerning the end consumer of the product or service that your business creates. For example, it can be interesting to look at where their influences are coming from in the form of social media, entertainment and leisure. What are their aspirations and preferences and how can your product or service be adapted to that? Trends concerning adoption of technology are the obvious example here.

Activity 9

If applicable to your organization, find out how what percentage of your sales come from consumers using a mobile device. Track this trend back over the last three years and obtain predictions from key stakeholders within your business on what they think the percentage will be for next year.

Then review the organizational structure for the areas of your business that support mobile growth and review over the same time period. Consider your predictions for how those business areas might need to change over the next 12 months in response to this trend.

Next, consider where that increase in sales has come from. Is this additional sales revenue coming from mobile or is this consumer trend leading to reduced sales in another area, eg bricks-and-mortar stores? Again, track back over the same period and see if you can correlate information here.

You will then need to consider your own predictions for how these other areas will change and reflect on what this may mean for workforce planning.

Relevance to HR

In Part Four of this book we will look specifically at trends impacting the future of HR, so our focus here is to look at how you can apply industry trend information in a way that is relevant to HR. In his book *Future Trends: A guide to decision making and leadership in business*, author Lawrence R Samuel categorizes future trends into six areas as follows:

1 cultural trends;

2 economic trends;

3 political trends;

4 social trends;

5 scientific trends;

6 technological trends.

This comprehensive list can serve to provide an effective framework for a trends map for HR. It is also essentially straightforward to implement and can apply across any industry or geography. The basic composition of this trends map is to initially identify the trend category, then define factors connected with this trend before moving on to articulate the potential impact on HR and then the potential impact in the business you operate in. An example of this can be found below.

Example trends map for HR

Trend Category 1: Cultural

Example: individualism – the growing trend for people to want to receive a more personalized commercial experience and to express their unique style and personality.

Impact on HR: to enable people to perform at their best, symptoms and working practices need to be developed to enable them to express their individualism at work and also to receive communication and data that feels personal to them.

Impact in this business: review dress codes and policies to enable a greater degree of self-expression, enabling individuals to bring their 'whole self' to work and for their unique skills and personality to shine.

Trend Category 2: Economic

Example: E-currency – a gradual shift towards digital currency becoming more mainstream and the use of cash declining.

Impact on HR: personal financial matters are one of the key disruptors affecting an individual's ability to perform and focus at work. The e-currency market is relatively easy and accessible for employees and due to its volatility at the moment has the potential to impact in a negative way if the individual goes into it poorly informed.

Impact in this business: consider establishing what percentage of employees are either actively engaged with or considering investing in e-currency and provide support through resources and educational material to enable improved decision making in this field.

Trend Category 3: Political

Example: instability – in uncertain and unprecedented times global and domestic political instability becomes more prevalent and with predictions that this isn't going away any time soon organizations need to ensure they are set up to navigate it.

Impact on HR: HR needs to stay on top of changes in thinking regarding policy and where possible engage with employer groups in their industry in order to leverage a commercial voice in political decision making.

Impact in this business: access to data and metrics will become key in order to establish the risks associated with policy changes and to scenario plan for the future. For example, if access to global talent is restricted, what impact will that have on talent acquisition? What percentage of the current workforce is migratory etc?

Trend Category 4: Social

Example: ageing population – with retirement ages rising and the potential that they may disappear altogether, combined with the fact that individuals are now living much longer than they ever have in history, this is a trend that is becoming of significant importance.

Impact on HR: older workers are already making a valuable contribution to business and this trend is set to continue. HR will need to ensure effective support for this group in order to maximize the commercial advantage they can bring.

Impact in this business: review talent acquisition strategy to ensure older workers do not receive discriminatory treatment. Establish reverse mentoring practices in order to enhance skills development across all demographics within the organization.

Trend Category 5: Scientific

Example: nanoscience – the study of all things at a nano, or one-billionth level, shifting focus to the super-micro level as opposed to the macro level.

Impact on HR: nano-designed products and techniques are on the increase in all industries. It can be interesting to map this concept across to HR. For example, a characteristic of nanoscience is to look at things from the bottom up as opposed to top down. If organizational goal setting is approached in the same way and evaluated against top-down goal setting, a more robust and sustainable plan may be created.

Impact in this business: review organizational goals and assess whether a bottom-up approach incorporating assessment at a nano level will add additional value to the relevance of the goals and the organization's ability to achieve them.

Trend Category 6: Technological

Example: artificial intelligence (AI) – the development and theory of computer systems being able to perform tasks that would normally be completed by humans, such as visual perception, speech recognition and decision making.

Impact on HR: AI technology is already being deployed effectively within Human Resources, specifically in the area of recruitment. In addition, chatbot technology is being deployed in HR service environments in order to provide a more personalized and efficient experience to employees.

Impact in this business: investigate opportunities to deploy chatbot technology in order to enhance the employee experience and create more efficient processes within HR.

Forecasting

According to the *Business Dictionary*, forecasting can be defined as 'A planning tool that helps management in its attempts to cope with the uncertainty of the future, relying mainly on data from the past and present and analysis of trends' (BusinessDictionary.com, 2018a).

The process typically starts with a number of assumptions based on information that has been collated within the business and also on the experience, knowledge and judgement of the leadership team. The assumptions can then be applied through a forecasting model which provides a framework for the analysis. There are a number of models that can be used for this purpose, with some of the most popular briefly summarized below:

- **Box-Jenkins.** This is a mathematical model based around looking at a specific time series and then forecasting data based on the information contained within that time series. Key factors taken into account are the stability of the time series and issues connected with seasonality of the data.

- **Delphi.** This model is essentially based on seeking information through consensus. It works by obtaining results through conducting several rounds of questionnaires and then obtaining anonymous responses that are then aggregated and shared with the group after each round. The participants completing the questionnaire are then permitted to amend their responses in subsequent rounds. Through the process of repeating the questionnaire and informing the participants of what the overall group thinks, this model progresses to reach a final, correct response through consensus.

- **Exponential Smoothing.** This is a statistical technique in which significant changes in data are detected through disregarding that which does not have any relevance to the purpose of the activity being conducted. A clear example of this is that in this process older data receives progressively less weight or importance and newer data is positioned with more importance. This technique can also be called averaging and is used when making short-term as opposed to long-term forecasts. 'The "wait-and-see" attitude to changes around them is the intuitive way people employ exponential smoothing in their daily living' (BusinessDictionary.com, 2018b).

- **Regression Analysis.** This process can be considered one of the most important forms of data analysis. A good example of how this is deployed can be looking at the subject of retail sales. Here we could consider that a store manager might be in a position where they are trying to estimate or predict the sales for the next month. In this they will be aware of the fact that there are a significant number of factors ranging from the weather, local events and promotional activity by competitors that will impact on the sales figures that can be achieved. Regression analysis is deployed in such scenarios in order to mathematically assess which of the variables has a real impact and to what extent.

Limitations

A key point to note regarding forecasting is that as this is a process that is founded to an extent on 'assumptions', the data that is produced from it can be prone to inaccuracies should the assumptions be off the mark. This becomes more of a possibility the further out a business attempts to forecast due to the high degree of factors that are difficult to predict, even up to projections for a five-year period. For this reason, forecasting and trend prediction will never be an exact science and the use of it should reflect that. Where it is used, it should form part of a holistic decision-making process.

Conclusion

Depending on the size of the organization you work in, trend and forecasting data will either be collated internally or via an external agency. When operating at a senior commercial level within the organization it will be essential for any HR practitioner to understand this data and the origin of it in order to be able to contribute to the strategic planning process. Through understanding the sources of this data, understanding its limitations and also how it is utilized, you will then be able to operate in a more credible way and upgrade the contribution you are able to make to the success of the business. A very effective way to do this is to create a trends map for HR in which you collate all of the research data that you have sourced both internally and externally and where you have articulated the potential impact of trends on both your function and the wider business. This can then be shared at a senior strategic level to support in driving progress and mitigating the risk that emerging trends might present to your organization.

Toolkit essentials: 5 steps to incorporate trend and forecasting information in your HR strategy

1 Establish a source of information that forecasts demographic information for the territories in which you employ people. Look at trends and predictions around unemployment levels, age demographics and consider any impact on your target talent pool.

2 Conduct research into high-performing universities and establish which of their courses are most likely to provide skills relevant to the future of your business; eg what are the most respected courses in relation to technology? Establish relationships with these universities and programme leaders now in order to tap into talent for the future.

3 Review your organization's position with regard to 'data science' and consider the option of strengthening the operation with the introduction of a Data Scientist role or by contracting in services to support in this area, depending on the scale of your organization.

4 Liaise with colleagues in product development and innovation and establish their source of trend and forecasting information. For example, this could be something like WGSN, a leading trend authority for fashion and lifestyle organizations. If your business already subscribes to such a service, investigate options for how you may also obtain access to this data.

5 Review social media platforms to ensure you are up to date with how they are being utilized by professionals in your industry. Consider YouTube, Twitter, Facebook and Instagram as starting points and search for keywords relating to your business and industry.

Questions for reflection

Q. What models for business forecasting are utilized in your organization?

Q. Who within your business is responsible for collating and communicating industry trend information?

Q. How do you keep yourself up to date with information relating to emerging trends in Human Resources?

References

BusinessDictionary.com (2018a) Business Forecasting, available at: www.businessdictionary.com/definition/forecasting.html [accessed 22 August 2018]

BusinessDictionary.com (2018b) What is exponential smoothing? Definition and meaning, available at: www.businessdictionary.com/definition/exponential-smoothing.html [accessed 22 August 2018]

Phillips, J (2018) The right way to try to predict the future, *Inc.*, available at: www.inc.com/jeffrey-phillips/the-right-way-to-try-to-predict-future.html?cid=search [accessed 22 August 2018]

Samuel, L (2018) *Future Trends: A guide to decision making and leadership in business*, Rowman & Littlefield

Where's the talent?

Introduction

In this chapter we explore the challenges of talent acquisition at industry level and emerging trends and factors that are reshaping the talent landscape. With technology as an enabler, organizations are now in a position where they are able to directly access a global pool of talent in a way that has not previously been possible. This brings significant opportunities and a platform to engage individuals; it also means that competition for talent is higher than ever before and that organizations need to up their game in order to remain competitive in this market.

How will this chapter shape my thinking?

- It will enhance your awareness of key trends impacting on talent acquisition.
- It will support you in evaluating sources of candidates in the industry in which you operate.
- It will encourage you to consider the role of recruitment agencies and how this may be evolving.

Emerging trends

Talent acquisition is perhaps one of the areas of HR that is most susceptible and responsive to emerging trends. This is due to the volume of interaction with individuals who operate outside of the organization and the weight of expectation connected to this, in addition to the commercial impact and expectations arising from within the business. In this area it's not only issues of technological development that come into play, it's also important to consider changing cultural norms and attitudes.

I spoke to Janine Jenkinson, Head of Talent Acquisition and Retail HR at River Island, and she considers the following three trends to be of particular importance in this area:

1 The use of artificial intelligence – we live in an age where people want things quickly and that is the same for recruitment. If you are working in a high-volume recruitment environment, things like chatbots need to be included; answers need to be immediate to support and improve the candidate experience. This couples well with the use of technology in recruitment, having a good applicant tracking system (ATS) that does so much of the hard work for you and dovetails in with your employer brand proposal.

2 The role of a recruiter – gone are the days when you used to post an advert on various job boards and sit back and wait for the response; the role of a recruiter is now more like a marketeer. You have to think about product placement, using those marketing messages to tie into your recruitment campaigns, and use that marketing data as a talent market map. It's important to consider where the recruitment message is positioned along with the product message.

3 Having an Agile approach to work/life balance – we are seeing an increase in candidates setting the tone for where and when they want to work and as an employer we need to embrace this to capture the top talent. Combined with this challenge is the internal education piece around hiring managers being brand ambassadors, selling the company and role to the candidate, which means that the balance of power is shifting. Experience is overshadowed in some cases by brand fit, which makes finding the right fit tough from a recruitment perspective.

Katrina Collier, social recruiting trainer, keynote speaker and founder of The Searchologist (www.thesearchologist.com) expands on this and identifies the following trends:

1 The continued battle to get attention – I don't believe we are in a war for talent, it's actually a fight for attention. There are four billion people generating an incredibly large amount of data and it's overwhelming. Recruiters who continue to 'spray and pray', thinking of social media as a job board, will continue to be ignored. Candidate ghosting is now very real and any wonder when recruiters have been ghosting people for years! Recruiters need to become skilled sourcers and people (candidate) engagement experts or they really could be replaced by robots.

2 Companies finally taking candidate experience seriously – I yearn for a time when I won't see 'never heard back' in interview reviews on Glassdoor! Just like recruiters who look at people all day, people look at recruiters and companies before they reply or apply. Eighty-six per cent won't apply to a company with a bad reputation so it's essential that companies look after their employees and their candidates, and show it! People want peer-to-peer authentic rich media and to feel inspired to hit that apply button.

3 Google for Jobs – 90 per cent of searches are run on Google and Google for Jobs delivers a better experience for job seekers by reducing duplicate posts and reducing the impact of job board aggregators like Indeed. In the United States it's already been shown to benefit companies by raising the visibility of the jobs on their own career sites. Each listing shows where the job is posted, giving the job seekers the choice as to where to apply, and the listings also show Glassdoor, Indeed, Kununu and other reviews and salary information sourced from sites like LinkedIn, Glassdoor, Payscale, job boards etc. The transparency and the ability to filter out agencies are game changers.

Artificial intelligence

Specifically on the topic of artificial intelligence, Collier goes on to add:

Maybe I am harsh but it's overhyped. Right now, they have a long way to go. Technology should always be used to assist recruiters, never to replace. What we do is so incredibly important – we play with people's lives! And I don't believe technology will ever be able to do that alone. The skills a recruiter needs to be successful include emotions that technology is yet to replicate like curiosity and empathy. Plus, 50 years since the first ATM (cashpoint) we still have tellers in banks because people like the human touch for something as mundane as withdrawing money. Do we really think people wouldn't want human support for something as important as their career?

Jenkinson also expands on her comments in relation to AI, noting:

I believe that it has a place and for volume campaigns it is a given – when you are working within the retail industry, heavy Christmas recruitment campaigns need AI to keep the pace and demand whilst delivering a seamless candidate experience. However, I firmly believe there will always need to be that human intervention – for roles where you need to target passive talent, the human factor is essential. AI can support the end goal but it won't totally eradicate a Talent team.

Market mapping

When considering the talent pool at industry level it is still common practice to engage in some form of market mapping activity either in-house or through engaging external support. In this process competitor organizations are identified and research completed which maps out individuals operating in key positions within these organizations.

Janine Jenkinson finds that market mapping does have limitations in that it is a constantly moving picture which can make effective reporting on it tough. She also notes that in her experience any market mapping that has been done internally has worked better than paid research. She observes:

Tools like LinkedIn are useful but the best way to create a credible map has been to use the knowledge that you already have in your business for your competitors. However, keeping this market map up to date is the tough job and in some cases for areas like Buying and Merchandising, this can be a full-time job!

Sources for talent acquisition

In this area it's also essential to maintain awareness of changing trends with regards to sources of talent and to ensure appropriate tracking mechanisms are in place to record this.

Janine Jenkinson's view is that sources of great candidates are changing. She notes:

> Sending messages to candidates/passive candidates through LinkedIn does work but only 50 per cent of the time; people are not sitting on LinkedIn all day waiting for a message and if they have a good background and experience, they will have a message from you and 25 of your competitors. Gone are the days of people applying for roles. I have seen a massive decline over the years of candidates actively searching for a role; CV databases on job boards are depleting. Candidates expect to be contacted on LinkedIn and then 'sold' the job! Therefore, to get the good people through the door, that initial contact and first meeting needs to retain a certain element of informality. Referrals from new hires are a fantastic way of getting good people but that means the new starters process needs to be brilliant – are you really going to refer an old colleague or friend to a company where your experience has been rubbish?! Driving the message of brand ambassadors and hiring managers networking to help find talent is the key. It is no longer okay to simply say 'recruitment can't find us anyone' – we all have a role to play to engage great talent but this then filters back to our employees being actively engaged.

Katrina Collier's view on the changing sources of candidates is:

> People are everywhere – recruiters are on LinkedIn. There are count-less tutorials on YouTube that teach how to find people online; it's easy to find people and that's the problem. Recruiters find people, shoot them an impersonal e-mail/InMail and expect a reply.

This spamming is the reason that the sources of great candidates are changing; people with skills that are in demand rarely log into LinkedIn. LinkedIn usage is down due to LinkedIn selling our data to recruiters and recruiter behaviour. So now I teach recruiters how to use the countless other sources of active users like Facebook's 2.14 billion, Instagram's 1 billion, Twitter's 440 million, and niche sites like Behance, GitHub, Stack Overflow, Meetup, Dribbble, and many more, but I place the emphasis on teaching recruiters and sourcers how to engage people. This involves hyper-personalization, respectfulness, manners, an extra moment of time, and looking like a company and recruiter worthy of someone's time – the latter is overlooked the most.

Recruitment agencies

In light of ongoing developments in talent acquisition, it can be interesting to consider the future of recruitment agencies. Janine Jenkinson predicts, 'I think there will always be a need for agencies; some candidates prefer having that middle man to help them, especially when it comes to negotiating salary and package.' This is a valid observation and even with the emergence of more social forms of recruitment and visibility of talent through platforms such as LinkedIn, there is no escaping the fact that experienced external recruiters still have a valuable role to play in securing the talent at the end of the process and negotiating packages. Jenkinson adds that where recruitment agencies are deployed, a partnership approach is key, where the recruiters within the agency are provided with a degree of information that enables them to understand the culture of the business in addition to the operational requirements of a role. She notes that 'Randomly sending CVs to companies without any knowledge of the business won't open doors for them.' Where an organization has a strong talent acquisition team in place it's likely that they will only resort to utilizing an agency when they are confident that they have exhausted their existing channels for sourcing people. This is a balance, though, and needs to be approached with a lens of commerciality where workload and existing priorities are considered in order to secure the best talent in the most effective way. Shifts in talent acquisition practices and technology do mean that in a lot of cases, organizations are now giving a lesser role to agencies and sourcing candidates via other means instead. Jenkinson notes:

> Agencies need to offer something different to the client. Everyone can use LinkedIn, job boards, CV databases – they need to demonstrate how they can find the hard-to-reach people and realize that sometimes the client won't want to work with them just because they have worked with our competitors.

Katrina Collier's view is:

> Many companies have successfully shifted away from over-reliance on agencies and built in-house recruitment functions, which is beneficial in so many ways on top of the obvious cash savings, so I see this continuing to happen. I have also seen the rise of what I call 'mini recruitment process outsourcers' (RPOs) where companies pay an executive search recruiter a fixed monthly figure to be their outsourced recruiter rather than working with agencies on a contingency basis. As mentioned above, Google for Jobs means agents need to be more transparent on location and salary, and build a better candidate reputation and experience to succeed. I believe the super niche candidate-centric agent recruiters will succeed along with those who deal in the low-level temp or high-end executive roles. But the majority of roles are mid-level and companies can do those very effectively with a bit of training.

Conclusion

In an area impacted so heavily by developments in technology there is no escaping the fact that human interaction and a personal touch are here to stay. We see technology very much as an enabler to human practice and performance and can observe that the best results are achieved when people feel appreciated, valued and recognized as individuals throughout the talent acquisition process. It could be argued that for at least the short term, the most significant developments in the field of talent acquisition will come from the use of social media and therefore the issues arise of how savvy recruiters are with this and how able they are to utilize it in a non-invasive way.

Toolkit essentials: 5 steps to assessing the viability of your sources for talent acquisition

1 Establish and map out all of the sources currently used for talent acquisition in your organization.

2 Determine which sources generate the highest volume of candidates.

3 Next, consider which sources generate the greatest volume of 'quality' candidates. If you don't already have measures to quantify 'quality of hire' you may need to integrate this at this stage.

4 When you have identified a measure to enable you to determine what constitutes a 'quality hire', identify individuals who meet this criterion who have joined the business in recent months. Survey them to determine which social media channels they are most engaged with and what time of day they are most likely to be active on social media.

5 Target recruitment activity so that it is aligned with the social media habits of high-performing, quality hires.

Questions for reflection

Q. How do you keep pace with emerging trends in talent acquisition in your industry?

Q. What social media channels do you currently recruit through?

Q. How do you currently map the market for talent in your industry?

Q. How do you plan to utilize AI in talent acquisition?

Workforce planning 21

Introduction

In this chapter we turn our focus to workforce planning, an essential business process integral to ensuring that the changing needs of the organization are aligned with the people strategy. When done well, workforce planning reflects the size and maturity of the business and brings together industry and market data to support a strategic planning process. It becomes an enabler to business performance and determines whether or not an organization will achieve the goals it has set.

How will this chapter shape my thinking?

- It will help you identify ways to avoid panic hiring and unnecessary redundancies.
- It will encourage you to evaluate the role of the wider leadership team in workforce planning.
- It will support you in assessing the role of technology in workforce planning.

The process

The process for workforce planning can be categorized in four steps as shown in Figure 21.1.

Figure 21.1 Key steps in workforce planning

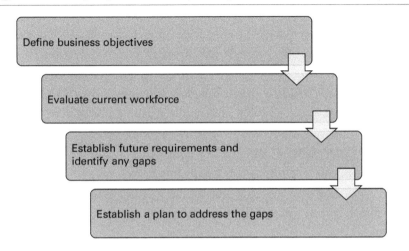

1 Define business objectives

As a starting point it is essential for business objectives to be articulated in order to provide clarity to the workforce planning process. This can be done in the form of a strategy, a vision, mission and goals at a top level and then broken down further to obtain additional detail at division and business function level. It is then possible to develop a strategic people plan which aligns with these objectives. In addition, by extending the objective identification to divisional level it's also possible to pick up on any incongruencies and establish if any sub-narratives and plans exist at idea conception or proposal stage that may impact on the overall direction of the business and workforce planning requirements. When objectives are identified it is then possible to determine what core competencies and skills will be required in which areas in order to support the growth of the business and drive it forwards.

The business objectives can then be considered in the context of talent development, talent acquisition and then finally gaps and risks. With regard to talent development, the identified objectives will indicate what learning interventions and programmes will need to be developed in order to provide the required skills mix for the business. It will also provide insight into how top performers should be identified and motivated in order to retain them. In relation to talent acquisition, defining the objectives will highlight how the recruitment strategy will need to evolve in order to find, assess and locate the right talent that will be essential to ensuring that the goals of the organization can be achieved. Through this process gaps will begin to emerge and present the question of how the organization should mitigate any skills shortages resulting from business repositioning and growth.

Other important factors that may arise from this process are likely to link to issues surrounding location, mode of operation and projected increases or decreases in volume of work.

For this reason, defining business objectives is an essential first step in workforce planning and one that should be invested in to ensure any plans created are of the highest quality and will be an accurate tool essential to support business growth.

2 Evaluate the current workforce

The second step involves ensuring that you have an accurate picture of the current workforce and trends within the organization. This enables you to evaluate the gap between the future requirements of the business and the current reality. From this, it is then possible to establish an effective gap-closing strategy. In order for this process to be effective it is essential for the HR professionals who are conducting this activity to have access to robust data and analytics concerning the current workforce. This data should include the following information:

- Employee data, including demographics, salary information, employment type, length of service and distribution of employees per division.
- Labour turnover statistics per division and role type.
- Recruitment data, including time to hire, sources of hire, quality of hire and cost per hire.
- Competency measures which distinguish skills and abilities of the current workforce and track progress of development activities.
- Reward data such as information on how employees at different levels are recognized and rewarded for their work.

- Utilization of contract workers should be clearly measured and articulated, as should fluctuations in any supplementary temporary workers.

It's also important to note that this should not be a purely desk-based activity. The real value here comes from combining the data with intelligence and insight from key influencers and decision makers in the business who may have additional context connected with pending budget changes, market influences and proposed structural changes that are not immediately obvious. Where possible it is also beneficial to obtain insight into competitor organizational structures and talent acquisition trends in order to maintain an effective map of external influences and challenges to talent retention.

3 Establish future requirements and identify any gaps

The data relating to the current workforce can be evaluated against the future business requirements identified from the business objectives identified in step 1. This should be worked through on a division-by-division basis and then a holistic top-level summary mapped for the organization. This gap analysis should include predicted areas of skills shortage, areas where headcount is predicted to reduce, labour turnover rates, succession planning predictions, talent acquisition metrics predicting time to hire and cost per hire, and correlation of activity with business objectives.

4 Establish a plan to address gaps

An effective plan to close the gaps should be an essential part of any HR strategy as this is key to increasing the capability, capacity and productivity of the workforce. It is possible to get some measure of this through utilizing predictive analytics and deploying forecasting techniques as detailed in Chapter 19, but the plan should be worked through in collaboration with key stakeholders and verified by the senior leadership team. The plan should identify which areas need to be addressed in which priority order in order to best support the business objectives. The strategy should include measures to recruit and retain the best-quality employees for the business and then also ensure that the processes and operational structure of the business are such that they then enable those individuals to deliver great work and operate at peak performance levels.

The role of the leadership team

The leadership team for the organization should play an active role in the workforce planning process. They have a primary responsibility for outlining the objectives for the organization and ensuring that these objectives are articulated well and communicated to all of the relevant stakeholders throughout the organization. In addition they should also play an active role in championing workforce planning activity in order to secure buy-in from the wider organization and therefore build trust in the process. Then, importantly, they need to instigate and support action deriving from the gap analysis and workforce plan, supporting this down through divisional level in order to ensure that action is taken quickly and work is prioritized where necessary.

Impact of technology

It can be suggested that the deployment of new technology in order to support workforce planning activities can enable organizations to access new levels of innovation and growth. In fact, it could be argued that it is now an essential factor in determining the success of the process, particularly with the evolution of changing ways of working such as gig work, virtual contracting and employment beyond retirement. It's important to remember, though, that any technology deployed should be considered as a tool to facilitate the process as opposed to something that can effectively automate it without the requirement for human interaction.

In addition, it's important to note the requirement for investment in technology and systems that can effectively provide HR teams with data and analytics to support the process. It will be very hard for HR to provide accurate budget and planning projections without reliable data available to them. It can often be the case that investment in this area is held back or delayed through prioritization of systems enhancements that are perceived as being more immediately commercial; however, this can prove to be a costly mistake in the long term, particularly in scenarios where a competitor has established systems and processes that are more readily able to provide the intelligence required.

Conclusion

Workforce planning is a core component of any effective HR strategy and should be intrinsically linked to the overall company strategy and objectives. Any plan created will only ever be as good as the data that has been collated to inform it and for that reason it is essential to combine data and analytics with insight from key stakeholders and decision makers within the organization. The most effective workforce plans are those that are created in collaboration with the leadership team and championed by them in both the process of collating the data that defines them and the action that results from them. Plans should be reviewed and adjusted regularly as new information comes to light arising from both internal and external sources. The plan should be considered a live document that moves and flexes in alignment with the objectives and performance of the organization.

Toolkit essentials: 5 steps to ensuring senior team buy-in with workforce planning activity

1 Involve senior leaders early on in the workforce planning process.

2 Clearly articulate the benefits expected from effectively completing the process.

3 Be prepared to articulate what will happen if workforce planning is not conducted on a regular basis.

4 Ditch the jargon. Ensure you articulate the process and benefits in commercial terms that are familiar to your business.

5 Establish a mechanism for co-creation of the workforce planning process and plan.

Questions for reflection

Q. Which skills and competencies will your organization need in the future that it doesn't have today in order to remain competitive?

Q. If no changes were made to the environment which houses your largest group of employees, how long would it remain a viable location, given projected increases or decreases in the workforce population?

Q. What percentage of your workforce is made up of contract workers?

PART FOUR
Know your profession

Professional accreditation

22

Introduction

In this chapter we turn our focus to the matter of professional accreditation within the HR profession and consider the ongoing relevance and credibility of this. In the UK the accrediting body for the profession is acknowledged as being the Chartered Institute of Personnel and Development (CIPD). Another professional body worth investigating is the Human Resources Certification Institute (HRCI) in the United States; established in 1976, it is considered to be the largest HR certification organization in the world. In addition, the Society for Human Resource Management (SHRM) is regarded as being the world's largest HR professional society, representing 300,000 members in more than 165 countries.

How will this chapter shape my thinking?

- It will encourage you to consider your motives for achieving professional accreditation.
- It will prompt you to consider the topic of recertification and continuous development.
- It will encourage you to devise alternative mechanisms to demonstrate your professional credibility.

Purpose of accreditation

When we consider the purpose of becoming accredited in a profession, in many industries the outcome is clear. Accreditation provides an indication to a consumer of the degree of professional competence of an individual from whom they are commissioning a service. This is no different in the context of HR. A professional qualification and chartered membership serve to offer a measure of comfort that the individual is suitably educated and qualified to do the job. Therefore, we as HR professionals endorse this process and measure of competence and this serves as the purpose that drives our desire to achieve a certain grade or level. It could, however, be argued that not all individuals who carry the same level of professional accreditation possess the same level of skill and competence. Therefore, other factors need to be considered both for the consumer or employer who engages the individual on the basis of perceived skill and also for the individual who needs to find a platform to showcase their skill and maintain credibility in a potentially crowded marketplace.

Recertification and continuous personal development

The first thing to consider here is the concept of recertification. Interestingly this is a process that is integral to the HRCI accreditation process but not currently a measure applied by the CIPD. The premise is that in order to maintain a particular designation or accreditation level the individual must undertake ongoing development activities that qualify for recertification credits. This ensures that professional competence is maintained and that the individual continues to upskill themselves in connection with the latest developments and trends. In the case of the CIPD, continuous professional development is encouraged but not essentially managed in the same way.

It is clear to see how mandatory recertification would drive ongoing development of individuals within the procession and further serve to support and improve the credibility of the HR profession.

In addition, it can help raise standards overall and make it easier for employers to identify candidates for roles who are more commercial, more progressive and committed to keeping their skills and knowledge up to date. There is certainly a risk of complacency with an accreditation framework that enables someone to achieve a certain level of accreditation (FCIPD, for example) and then do nothing beyond that point to ensure they are updating their skills and keeping up to speed with new developments. This not only results in a situation that is damaging for the profession but also does nothing to help the individual.

It is, however, acknowledged that this is not necessarily an easy thing to change and where perhaps an ideal would be to introduce mandatory recertification for all grades of accreditation this could be done in stages and would need to be tested and pioneered before introducing it on perhaps a mandatory basis for new members joining the profession and on an elective basis for existing members. This would ensure a gradual cultural change supported and driven by ambassadors who are fully committed and bought in to the process with the desire to further elevate the perception of HR.

Essentially, this would be a move to a position where CIPD members earn recertification credits for development activities, for example training courses, attendance at seminars and events, speaking engagements, online learning, mentoring programmes etc. The recertification period would be between two and three years, tracked digitally in a similar way to the system currently deployed by the HRCI. In addition and linked to the above, core commercial skills training could be introduced to the qualifications framework and also recognized as a CPD activity for recertification. This could include financial planning skills, project management, awareness of e-commerce and digital technology, and also recognition for secondments or commercial experience obtained in business areas outside of HR.

Where this approach may only be an aspiration at this point in time there is a way that any professional operating in HR today can adopt this mindset should they choose to do so and the most accessible way to do this is through continuous personal development (CPD) activity. We touch on this further in Chapter 26 where our focus is professional development.

At the moment, we are in a position where the same conversations keep cropping up time after time about HR and business credibility. It's time for this to stop and time for us to move forward – and to do that we need action and change. We need to do something different to break the cycle and get a different result. Part of this links with our qualification, CPD and accreditation framework and part of this is in the hands of every person working in HR today. It's time to be brave, take positive action and spend more time actively being the change we want to see instead of just talking about it. We all have a responsibility to be the best that we can be both for ourselves and for the future of HR. After all, we chose this as our profession and therefore need to take ownership for taking actions that will lead to progress and positive change.

Show don't tell

The second point to flag here is that there are a growing number of excellent HR professionals working today who do not possess a professional accreditation. We see this at all levels including executive level where it is possible for execs to transition from a non-HR background successfully into the lead HR role. So where a formal accreditation may be desired in order to demonstrate the appropriate level of education, experience and skill it most certainly is not always required. What is required, however, is the ability to demonstrate tangible results and commercial impact. In many ways the ability to provide clear evidence of this and that these results have been delivered on a consistent basis is more powerful than providing evidence of a certification. Commercial results really do speak for themselves and for that reason it is proposed that individuals turn their focus and efforts to this area so they may be in a position to let their work talk for them and practically showcase their ability to create action and make an impact in the organizations they support.

Conclusion

Professional accreditation still has a significant role to play for the majority of HR professionals who desire to operate at a strategic level today and there are a number of ways that accreditation can be achieved depending on the governing body responsible for the territory you operate in. In some areas recertification is mandatory and continues to drive professional competence. In cases where it is not mandatory, progressive individuals take it upon themselves to drive their development and undertake activities that ensure they remain relevant and able to impact at a strategic level. In all cases it is suggested that the end user of the services provided by HR values action, impact and results over 'letters after a name' or a dated certificate as a measure of competence. The most powerful thing we can do in order to demonstrate the impact of the work we can deliver is to act and to show it, not just talk about it. If people see for themselves the benefit and commercial advantage achieved through the work we deliver, in fact the concept of accreditation on a personal level almost becomes null and void as it's the results we achieve that truly provide a measure of how competent, skilled and educated we really are.

Toolkit essentials: 5 activities to complete in order to add more credibility to your professional accreditation

1   Read widely and ensure that you apply key information in your day-to-day activity. Cross-reference your reading with the accreditation framework for the CIPD and SHRM in order to accelerate your progress.

2   Map out your own personal development activity for the next 12 months. What skills will you build on or acquire and why?

3   Plan ahead for the next six months and book in relevant networking events that will enable you to engage with professionals who are at a more senior level than yourself or whose experience is more diverse.

4   At the end of each week reflect on where you have made a commercial impact in your organization. Look forward to the next week and identify opportunities for impact where you can 'show' your skill and competence in order to help move the business forward.

5 Consider how you can support in enhancing the perception and professional competence of the HR profession. If you're not already, what would it take for you to be proud to say you work in HR?

Questions for reflection

Q. If mandatory recertification was required for HR professionals would it change the way you approached your own development activity for this year?

Q. If professional accreditation didn't exist and you had to demonstrate your degree of skill through your results, what commercial results could you demonstrate from the past three months?

Q. What personal projects do you have landing over the next six months that will enable you to demonstrate commercial impact?

Responsibilities 23

Introduction

In this chapter our focus will be on exploring the responsibilities we take on when we embark on a career in HR. We will consider some of the traditional responsibilities associated with the role and also reflect on wider responsibilities that are not immediately obvious. In addition, we look at the challenges presented by these responsibilities and identify mechanisms through which these challenges can be overcome. It's fair to say that the responsibilities of individuals working in the HR profession are somewhat unique in that there are very few roles in the organization, particularly when you get to senior level, where responsibilities span all areas of the business and encompass all levels of employees. Then when you combine this with commercial, operational and strategic responsibilities it could be suggested that the only other role with a similar burden of responsibility is the CEO position of which, of course, HR aspires to be a strategic partner.

> **How will this chapter shape my thinking?**
>
> - It will encourage you to reflect on the responsibilities that comprise your role and assess what impact they have on your ability to contribute strategically to the organization you support.
> - It will prompt you to assess the additional responsibilities that you have acquired that are in addition to your core role and evaluate the impact of this additional workload.
> - It will encourage you to consider your responsibilities in relation to professional competence and development of the HR profession.

Core responsibilities

There are clearly some core responsibilities that are traditionally associated with the HR profession. These encompass providing support, services and strategic direction across the full range of the employee lifecycle across all divisions of the business you operate in. These responsibilities are combined with the requirement to strategically drive and support the organization in addition to providing sound counsel to executives and members of the leadership team. In addition, it is now essential for all HR professionals to embrace emerging core responsibilities that arise through the changing world of work, evolution of the profession and developments in technology.

When considering core responsibilities it is important to ensure alignment and synergy between what the HR function perceives these to be and the expectations of the wider organization and the business leadership team. This is particularly important as there will be variances in this between different organizations. As an example of this, *Entrepreneur* magazine states the following definition for the responsibilities of HR: 'The department or support systems responsible for personnel sourcing and hiring, applicant tracking, skills development and tracking, benefits administration and compliance with associated government regulations' (Entrepreneur, 2018). While this definition is of course true it is somewhat narrow in comparison to the wider remit that most strategic HR professionals aspire to.

Additional responsibilities

In addition to any existing core responsibilities it is becoming more and more common to see HR professionals expanding their reach into different areas and taking on additional requirements linked to this. In the case of additional responsibilities, there will be some that we naturally take upon ourselves because it serves a purpose for us to do so or because it is something that we feel personally invested in or passionate about. Then there will be additional responsibilities that will be given to you by other people throughout your career. In this context some will be given to you as development activities and some may well come your way because the perception in the business is that there is nowhere else for that responsibility to go and therefore it moves to HR. Therefore, on this point regarding additional responsibilities it is important to consider what it is that you are taking on and the reason for it.

Leadership responsibilities

When operating at a senior strategic level it is essential for any HR professional to be able to step up and contribute commercially across the entire organization. In order to do this, they have a responsibility to become connected and knowledgeable across all business areas. In addition, another key factor here is relationship management with peers and the board of directors. It should be noted that this is only possible where the leadership team of the organization is comfortable that their perceived expectations of HR responsibilities are being met. Failure to execute perceived core responsibilities with precision and efficiency will only result in them continuing to rear their head and effectively act as blockers to a level of more strategic contribution.

In addition, at all levels and particularly so at leadership level, HR has a responsibility to challenge and question – not always an easy task but essential if the business is to truly benefit from investment in the function. Indeed, there may well be situations that arise where the lead HR person is one of the only people who can effectively challenge at the most senior level, both with regard to matters connected with important business decisions and ethical practice, and also to hold a mirror up to senior and influential individuals where needed. Orlando Martins, Founder and CEO of Oresa Ltd, expands on this:

CEOs are looking for HR directors who are business-minded independent thinkers. They must be customer-centric, visionary leaders, willing to express their true opinion rather than being survivors who back initiatives they don't believe in. This is only possible if they are subject matter experts with the confidence to be courageous.

Responsibility to your profession

At the time of writing this book it's fair to say that the perception of HR is mixed and with the profession evolving at a faster rate than perception in some areas this particular point is of significance. It's important to say that if you have consciously or unconsciously chosen HR as your profession you have a responsibility to represent yourself and the profession in a way that positively reflects the work associated with it. The perception of the profession and its role won't change if the individuals representing the profession don't change within it. For this reason, we all have a responsibility to showcase and champion great work, not only to our peers within the profession but also on a wider stage to enable the external perception to change. In its simplest terms this can be explained as follows:

1 Do great work.

2 Share great work within the HR profession.

3 Champion and share the great work of other HR professionals.

4 Share and showcase great work outside of the HR profession.

5 Find ways to articulate the commercial results originating from HR activity.

One final point to make on the topic of professional responsibility is that of the requirement to find ways to give back to the profession. This can take many forms and could be something organized formally via a professional body such as the CIPD, either in terms of mentoring or branch support. Or it could be something organized on a personal level where you may seek out opportunities to give back in a way that resonates with yourself, potentially through blogging, social media activity, informal mentoring and coaching, and participation at events.

Conclusion

The scope of responsibility for HR professionals is vast and is a blended mix of those responsibilities given to us in a professional capacity and those which we take on ourselves both professionally and beyond. It is true that HR professionals do find themselves in something of a unique position with a remit that spans entire organizations and has an expectation of operational, commercial and strategic delivery combined with a required talent for facilitating performance of individuals up to and including C-suite level. In order to be truly effective at a strategic level, HR must extend beyond a remit of merely asking what should be done and what leaders would like to see done. The responsibility becomes one of co-creation and shaping that results in an integrated decision-making process which protects the business and enables it to achieve targets that have been set. In addition, it is important to remember that all HR professionals also have a responsibility to themselves as detailed in Part One of this book, where it is noted that in order to deliver excellence we need to operate from a position of excellence and in such a way that protects our own mental and physical wellbeing and promotes a position of continuous personal development.

Toolkit essentials: 5 steps to identifying responsibilities we should let go

1 List out all your responsibilities and arrange them in order of commercial impact.

2 Next to each activity estimate the percentage of your time you spend on that activity.

3 Highlight all areas where the commercial impact is low and the time commitment is high.

4 With low-impact, high-time-commitment activities, establish if they could be ceased, automated, delegated or reassigned.

5 Invest the recovered time in activities that generate a high commercial impact.

Questions for reflection

Q. What does the leadership team in your business consider to be the core and additional responsibilities of HR? (Avoid making assumptions here, collate info direct)

Q. What great work have you delivered that you could share with other professionals operating in HR?

Q. How and when could you showcase the value of HR to professionals operating outside of the profession?

Reference

Entrepreneur (2018) Human Resources definition, available at: www.entrepreneur.com/encyclopedia/human-resources [accessed 17 September 2018]

Advisory bodies and resources 24

Introduction

In this chapter our focus will be on advisory bodies for the HR profession and resources available to support delivery of the role. We reflect on the support available at personal, industry and professional level and how this combines as part of an effective toolkit for all HR professionals.

> ### How will this chapter shape my thinking?
>
> - It will prompt you to engage with appropriate advisory bodies at the relevant time in order to enhance your professional results.
> - It will encourage you to establish a network of resources as part of your professional toolkit that you can deploy as needed.
> - It will encourage you to question and challenge appropriately and position yourself in such a way that other professionals come to you as a source of advice and guidance.

Purpose

Professional advisory bodies exist in order to provide a consistent and respected source of information and guidance in the field they operate in. Typically they are multifaceted, providing resources both for organizations and individuals with a range of offerings suited to each audience. Their purpose could be defined as promoting good practice or excellence in a specific field or providing recommendations and suggestions for how things should be done, typically based on legislation and extensive research.

With this in mind it is important to say that 'good practice' has the potential to be a fairly contentious term and something to approach with caution and in accordance with the culture and landscape of the organization you work within. It is actually very hard to set one measure for 'good practice' on a specific topic where the scope and diversity of organizations and cultural alignment is so vast. Instead, it is perhaps best to remember that advisory bodies and external resources comprise only elements of process or research, which you will need to combine to reflect the nuances of the business you operate within. They are tools to deploy as opposed to end-to-end solutions and models for operation.

Industry

At industry level it is important to familiarize yourself with the appropriate advisory bodies relevant to that industry. As a starting point identify which advisory bodies exist and then research in order to become familiar with their services and, where relevant, membership requirements. Most professional advisory bodies have some mechanisms through which you will be able to participate in research or activities that will support you in making a difference in that industry, and also support you in raising your profile beyond the scope of the organization you work in. Some examples of this are as follows:

The Confederation of British Industry (CBI). The CBI promote themselves as being the UK's premier business organization. Their main proviso is that they provide a voice for firms at regional, national and international level with regard to informing and influencing policymakers.

British Retail Consortium (BRC). The BRC is the trade association for retailers in the UK with a purpose to shape debates, promote retail and influence issues that impact on this specific industry. Members of the consortium are therefore in a position where they can participate in activities which ultimately shape the industry in which they work and play a role in ensuring that the voice of industry is heard at the appropriate level in order to influence policy and decision making.

The US Chamber of Commerce. This is the world's largest business organization and represents the interests of more than 3 million businesses. They engage with organizations of all sizes, sectors, and regions effectively acting as their voice in Washington DC. In addition, The International Affairs Division of the US Chamber of Commerce leads the business community's efforts to shape global policy.

The Confederation of European Business. Known as BusinessEurope, this is the leading advocate for growth and competitiveness at European level, representing organizations across the continent. They position themselves as speaking for all-sized enterprises in 34 European countries whose national business federations are their direct members. The primary aim is to ensure that the voice of business is heard at European policy-making level.

Professional

In terms of advisory bodies for the HR profession we are fortunate enough to have a number of options and therefore can draw from more than one source in order to inform our decision making. In addition, our advisory bodies are accessible enough that professionals at all levels can obtain the guidance and professional support they require. In addition, and particularly in the case of the CIPD, membership enables individuals operating within the profession to be part of an organization that is recognized at industry level with regard to commenting on and shaping government policy.

It's fair to say that in the UK the CIPD is the most recognized advisory body for the HR profession, providing not only guidance and the learning and accreditation framework for the profession which we will explore later, but also providing members with tiered levels of involvement opportunities through which they can make an impact and shape the profession.

The Society for Human Resource Management (SHRM) operates in a similar way, predominantly across the United States but again with a global footprint that sees influence and activity beyond that.

The Advisory, Conciliation and Arbitration Service (ACAS) is another source of information and support both for employees and employers within the UK, providing information, advice, training, conciliation and other services to help prevent or resolve workplace problems. Whilst it can be a perception that ACAS only gets involved in scenarios of conflict resolution its service offer has expanded significantly over the past years to include a greater range of training courses, workshops and a free digital learning platform 'ACAS OnLine', providing a raft of valuable content both for individuals and employers alike.

Personal

It's also important to consider sources of advice on a personal level and in this regard the value of a professional mentor cannot be underestimated, regardless of the level of professional competence that has been achieved. We will cover this further in the next chapter relating to professional development but it is also worth flagging here as a valuable component to your 'resources' toolkit. In addition, with regard to resources available, on a personal level there has never been a time where so much information has been accessible to so many people in so many forms. Indeed, active participation in social media communities can provide a quick and reliable sounding board when developing ideas or compiling research for a project.

Conclusion

For any professional looking to improve their contribution to both the business and the industry they operate in it is essential to be aware of relevant advisory bodies and resources that operate in their field. This enables the professional to draw on these resources, ensuring that unnecessary work is avoided and 'good practice' principles can be considered in line with the culture and operating practices of the organization being supported. In addition, establishing a robust network of sources of support and information enables the HR professional to operate from an improved position of confidence and strength, therefore enabling further professional growth and competence. Further to this, engagement and participation in professional or trade associations and bodies enables individuals to make an impact way beyond personal and even organizational level, thus facilitating a more rewarding career and a platform from which the individual can make a lasting impact and instigate large-scale, meaningful change.

Toolkit essentials: 5 steps to increasing your involvement and profile with professional advisory bodies

1 Review the organization's website and establish if there is any guidance or direction on how individuals can get involved and play an active role in activities.

2 Review which social media channels the organization utilizes and actively engage in discussion through these channels.

3 Establish if there are any local groups or chapters connected to the organization that you could support with.

4 Reach out to other individuals who are already active in the organization in order to make a more personal connection that enables you to gain a greater understanding of how you may be able to get involved and also establish what format of involvement and contribution is right for you.

5 Stick with your commitments – if you do commit to getting more involved in supporting an advisory body be sure to respect that commitment and show up and deliver any work or support that you have promised.

Questions for reflection

Q. In what ways could you personally become involved in supporting advisory bodies in your industry?

Q. How could membership of a professional advisory body positively benefit the organization you work in at a strategic level?

Q. What advisory bodies exist that are most relevant to the organization and industry you work in?

Career framework

25

Introduction

In this chapter we will review potential career frameworks for HR professionals and consider the relevance of these in line with the evolving nature of the role. We will also consider how such frameworks support executives transitioning into the profession at a senior strategic level in addition to supporting the careers of individuals joining at entry level. We will look at the role of experience markers within a career framework and how non-linear progression can be a valuable component connected to professional success.

How will this chapter shape my thinking?

- It will encourage you to consider the CIPD Profession Map in the context of your own role and the HR function and organization that you work in.

- It will prompt you to assess your own competencies and those of your team in accordance with the SHRM Competency Model.

- It will encourage you to consider the experiences that form key milestones within a career framework and proactively plan to build exposure to such experiences as part of your own development activity.

CIPD framework

Launched in 2013, the CIPD Profession Map provided a framework through which individuals and organizations could benchmark HR capability both in terms of effectiveness and maturity and use this benchmark as a catalyst for progression. The 2013 map still retains its validity and relevance, but a new version was launched at the CIPD Annual Conference and Exhibition in 2018. This new map is positioned as being a mechanism to guide the HR profession into the future.

The 2013 map will be phased out, but the CIPD currently note that it is still relevant if you are currently studying (or thinking of studying) for a CIPD qualification or applying (or thinking of applying) for professional membership or experience assessment or upgrading. For that reason it is still referenced here. There are three components to the 2013 model as follows.

Professional areas

There are 10 professional areas with two core areas that sit at the very heart of the model:

- insights, strategy and solutions;
- leading HR.

The remaining eight areas are articulated as follows:

- organization design;
- organization development;
- resourcing and talent planning;
- learning and development;
- performance and reward;
- employee engagement;

- employee relations;
- service delivery and information.

Behaviours

There are eight behaviours identified in the map and each one is then described at four bands of professional competence. The behaviours identified are named as:

- curious;
- decisive thinker;
- skilled influencer;
- personally credible;
- collaborative;
- driven to deliver;
- courage to challenge;
- role model.

Bands

As detailed above, each behaviour is also divided into four bands of professional competence which reflect the hierarchy of the profession.

The new profession map is a great move on, placing *Purpose* at the centre and following it with three factors: *Principles-led*, *Evidence-based*, and *Outcomes-driven*. Next the new map articulates six areas of core knowledge which all HR professionals should become familiar with. It's here we see some great progression in relation to focusing on digital working and business acumen.

Next, we see eight core behaviours and again it's great to see commercial drive, passion for learning and situational decision making featuring here. Finally, the outer layer of the new map consists of nine areas of specialist knowledge which complete the model.

This is an incredibly comprehensive framework and arguably a gold standard map for defining required competence and skill for HR professionals. It will be interesting to observe its adoption over the coming years.

SHRM competency model

SHRM has a competency model for HR which comprises nine competencies, defined as follows:

- human resource expertise (HR Knowledge);
- ethical practice;
- leadership and navigation;
- business acumen;
- consultation;
- critical evaluation;
- communication;
- global and cultural effectiveness;
- relationship management.

(SHRM, 2016.)

Each competency then incorporates a number of sub competencies, behaviours and proficiency standards. In addition, in a similar format to the CIPD Profession Map, the SHRM framework incorporates four levels of competence, specifically 'Early Level', 'Mid Level', 'Senior Level', and 'Executive Level'. Competencies are then grouped together in clusters to support with targeting development objectives and driving progression through the professional levels. The SHRM framework is very accessible and easy to interpret, again proving to be a gold standard measure of how to operate in an HR role.

PX model framework

In earlier chapters we considered the concept of a 'People Experience (PX)' delivery model for HR, noting that it comprised the following four pillars:

- happiness and wellbeing of people;
- smart use of data and technology;
- commercial and evidence-based practice;
- focus on the future of work.

We then established that for maximum commercial impact, delivery of work streams in each pillar should be enabled through the deployment of Agile working practices and project management, very much with an emphasis on co-creation of work and meaningful work being released in iterations in order for enhanced commercial value to be achieved.

It is valuable to connect this here from the perspective of the impact this has on an HR career framework. At this stage it is important to acknowledge that both the CIPD and SHRM frameworks are equally relevant and valid to ensuring professional competence and therefore are valuable components of a career framework focusing on the PX model of delivery. However, to truly optimize results here it is suggested that further development activity and learning will need to be integrated in order to enable effective delivery of the PX model.

It is my suggestion that this be done through structuring development activity in line with the four knowledge areas that comprise this book, specifically in relation to:

- knowing yourself;
- knowing your business;
- knowing your industry; and
- knowing your profession.

As an example of this we could look at the knowledge area of 'knowing yourself' and connect this with the pillar of 'happiness and wellbeing of people'. Then, considering this on a personal level as we discussed in Chapter 1 with regards to your own development, it is then possible to evaluate your current level of strength and competence in this area and devise a plan for how you can build your own mental strength and self-care in order to improve the commercial contribution you are able to make and the value you can add in your role. This effectively becomes part of your ongoing continuous professional development activity.

Then we could consider the knowledge area of 'knowing your business' and map this across to the pillar of 'commercial and evidence-based practice', prompting you to integrate activities and experiences that enable you to have a commercial view across the entire organization with that view backed by sound evidence and knowledge. With regard to this point, I would actively encourage all HR professionals to take up a secondment in another business area should the opportunity arise to do so, or to transition out of HR altogether into another business function before returning back to HR at a later point. There is no substitute for this as a mechanism for improving your operational business knowledge and the experience of working outside HR as part of your career plan will enable you to return to the profession with a more commercial viewpoint and a level of experience you would otherwise have not achieved.

Non-linear experience markers

Regardless of what level you come into the profession at there is one thing that remains consistent: the sooner you start to build up real experiences of doing the job the better. It's clear to see that both the CIPD map and the SHRM model have tiers of progress through the desired competencies or behaviours and indeed this is exactly what you would expect to see in any competency model. However, it's also important to consider something I refer to as 'non-linear experience markers' as they can have a significant impact on progression through a career framework and on a professional's ability to deliver results in their role. It is my proposal that the conscious planning of these experience markers can significantly accelerate progression and ensure a sustained level of success, particularly in relation to commercial delivery. To highlight how this works I relate this to an example connected with the career map for a retail store manager.

Predominantly all retail managers follow a similar career path and that is that they start out as a sales assistant or customer service operative and then gradually work their way up through the hierarchy before reaching the management role, eg senior sales assistant, supervisor, floor/department manager, assistant/deputy manager and then store manager, maybe even then going on to general manager depending on the structure of the business and the size of store. It's rare for there to be a defined time period for this but very often competencies exist where certain skills need to be developed and demonstrated in order to progress to the next level. All being well and without any event causing disruption to the process this can work well and set people up for success. However, the reality can be that things don't always go to plan and particularly in phases of rapid growth and scaling individuals can find themselves in management positions without following a defined competency structure. So this is where the concept of curating non-linear experience markers come into play. What we may say is that we select a host of experiences that need to be included in the career framework for an individual in this field as part of the journey to becoming a store manager. Their experiences are identified up front and in reality could occur in any one of the behavioural or competency tiers. In our example of the retail manager, a selection of these experience markers could be as follows:

- work for a period of three months or more in a high-performing store;
- be part of a team opening a new store;
- lead or participate in the turnaround of an underperforming store;
- be involved in a store refit;
- spend two weeks shadowing a member of staff in the marketing team;
- work on a cross-functional project at company level.

This can also be considered in relation to the HR profession through identification of non-linear experiences that support the existing frameworks and further accelerate professional competence.

For example, 'experience markers' that you may wish to consider as part of your own career framework could be as follows:

- take a secondment in a non-HR function or take a commercial role outside of HR for a period of 12 months or more;
- involvement in a cross-functional project relating to commercial delivery through the deployment of enhancements to technology;
- working in a 'start-up' environment;
- operating in a stand-alone role;
- working in a unionized environment;
- undertaking an international assignment.

Conclusion

As HR professionals, we are fortunate to have comprehensive models which map out a potential career framework for us. These models apply regardless of level of entry into the profession and are founded on significant research and investment. However, they will only ever be as good as the way in which we deploy them and how we utilize them. As the profession evolves it is important to consider the evolution of these frameworks, particularly in relation to the mental strength and wellbeing of HR professionals and also the changing requirements of the role connected with deployment of new technology and automation. The introduction of non-linear experience markers across competency levels and bands serves further to set professionals up for success and beyond and provides stepping stones for an individual from which they can map out progress towards a defined career aspiration.

Toolkit essentials: 5 steps to utilizing the PX model as part of your own career development framework

1 Start by listing out the four pillars of the PX model – happiness and wellbeing, smart use of data and technology, commercial and evidence-based action, and focus on the future of work.

2 Next, under each heading identify one thing you can do in the next 30 days to improve your performance and/or competence in relation to that pillar.

3 Take your four actions and re-list them in priority order with the thing that will have the most commercial impact at the top. (Note that this may well be a self-care activity if it enables you to deliver results from an improved position of strength and resilience.)

4 Next, with each action, write a date for when you will have completed that activity.

5 Transfer the information across to whatever diary or planning tool you currently use and then map back in the days preceding the completion date to factor in any prep work or research that you may need to do before then.

Questions for reflection

Q. What development activity would you need to undertake today if you wanted to broaden your remit beyond HR six months from now?

Q. Which career framework for HR do you associate most with and how can you utilize it in order to progress?

Q. What is your career aspiration and linked to this what 'experience markers' do you need to plan in to accelerate your progress towards it?

References

CIPD (2018) Profession Map FAQs, available at: www.cipd.co.uk/learn/career/profession-map/faqs [accessed 2 October 2018]

SHRM (2016) SHRM Competency Model, available at: www.shrm.org/LearningAndCareer/Career/Pages/shrm-competency-model.aspx [accessed 2 October 2018]

Professional development

26

Introduction

In this chapter our focus is on your own professional development and we bring together some of the themes we have explored in earlier chapters as we look at what it really takes to ensure your career progresses in the way you want it to. In comparison to the concept of 'personal' development, 'professional' development is where we have a deeper-dive focus into an area of specialism connected to your career as opposed to a holistic programme of development which is multi-faceted and comprises elements that often do not relate to your chosen profession and work.

How will this chapter shape my thinking?

- It will prompt you to consider the impact of key influencers and future shapers on your own professional development.

- It will encourage you to think about the impact of procrastination on your career plan.

- It will encourage you to proactively work through scenarios where you start to doubt your professional career choices.

Know your profession

In the final part of this book our focus has been on knowing your profession and this should not be overlooked as a key foundation for your professional development. Invest time in really understanding the different responsibilities and roles associated with the profession you have chosen and you can then determine where your interest lies. You may choose to specialize in a particular area or operate as a generalist with potential to oversee all specialisms. In addition, this is particularly relevant for professionals transitioning into HR at a senior strategic level from another discipline. Taking time to invest in familiarizing yourself with the existing structures and operating models of HR then enables you to shape what you would like it to become in the context of the organization you are supporting and with the added value of the strategic background you bring from your original profession. In addition, through immersing yourself in your profession, additional development activities and opportunities can arise from becoming involved in activities outside of the organization you work in that will support in enhancing your professional reputation and increasing trust in the quality of your work. In an article that appeared in *Forbes* magazine, Ahyiana Angel, the host of 'Switch, Pivot or Quit', a podcast in which she shares her insights to help businesswomen decide if they should switch, pivot or quit their jobs, observes that through establishing a reputation outside of an organization the employee's value within a company is increased and internal confidence in the individual is boosted. She notes that 'You will develop influence as a by-product and opportunities to shine will naturally come your way without you constantly having to push your agenda' (Carter, 2018).

Professional derailers

With total certainty I can promise you that there will come a point where you will question if HR is the right profession for you. This might happen in response to a particular situation that arises or it could creep up on you over time in a less obvious way. Know that this is totally normal and provides a great inflection point from which you can assess how far you have come and set out your vision for the future. Operating from this position can result in a scenario where you are not able to deliver your best work and remaining in that position can impact on your confidence, your reputation and your physical and mental health. For that reason, it is useful to explore some of the potential causes of this and identify how these scenarios can be best navigated.

Health and wellbeing

This is perhaps the most important factor and often the most overlooked in terms of a professional derailer. Your health has a direct impact on your ability to perform and when you neglect it, or when a health matter arises that needs to be dealt with it can mean that everything else has to stop until this matter has been resolved. There are of course some things that we can't, anticipate, control or change about our health, but there are steps we can take in order to mitigate the risk of this becoming a derailer to professional development. Specifically, take steps to ensure you are fuelling your body appropriately for the performance level you hope to achieve. Then, take whatever form of exercise works best for you in order to maintain good levels of personal health and wellbeing. Finally, be quick to follow up and take action if you have a health concern. It can be tempting to put this off, often because we feel we are too busy, but the long-term consequences of this can ultimately result in you having to take a longer period of time out and have a longer and more protracted impact on your professional development.

Passion and alignment

As we explored in Chapter 2, in order to be in a position where you can really excel and deliver your best work it certainly helps to be passionate about the work you are doing and for your skills and talents to be aligned with it. This can be an easy one to spot when it starts to become an issue as it's incredibly hard to 'fake' passion and therefore people around you tend to pick up on it quickly. As with anything, it is natural to expect that passion may fade over time if you don't do things to keep that passion alive. So, if you are in a position where you are not as aligned with or passionate as you once were about your career choice there is a simple process you can follow to address this. First, remind yourself what attracted you to the career in the first place; establish if there is any action you can take now to reconnect you with the way you felt at that stage. Next, make a list of all of the elements of the role that you enjoy and which motivate you. Take action to reconnect with those elements and map out a 30-day plan for how you can do this. Then, make a list of all of the things that drain you and which you don't enjoy. Establish if there is any action you can take to improve the way you feel about those things and the impact they have on you. If you identify actions, take them immediately. This is a good exercise to determine the balance of things you are in alignment with in the job and the things you aren't. Finally, make a list of all of the things you are passionate about now and the things you consider to be non-negotiables in your career. As a final check, evaluate this against your current career choice and determine if your real passion and values are in line with the profession you have chosen.

Confidence

It doesn't matter how far you progress in your career, it's still possible to have your confidence knocked at any level. This can be due to finding yourself in situations that you were not adequately prepared for, destructive leadership practices, lack of support and guidance, and even fear stemming from previous negative experiences. In situations where your confidence has become a professional derailer one of the most effective solutions to this is to find a mentor who you respect and who has achieved the type of results that you aspire to achieve as your career progresses. In addition, where confidence has become a factor it can be important to re-set and start to rebuild it through cultivating some small wins in areas where you do feel more confident, with the aim of building momentum and positivity which will map across to any areas of concern.

Continuous professional development (CPD)

It can be easy to get left behind if you don't focus on your own CPD, particularly with the rate of technological development and rapid growth of social media. Depending on the level at which you are operating this is more likely to be a derailer that builds slowly over time as opposed to one that immediately knocks your career off course. This is, however, one of the easiest professional derailers to fix and can be addressed by simply creating a format for a development plan that works for you. The professional accreditation frameworks we discussed in Chapter 22 are a great place to start with this. Then it could even be as simple as blocking out time in your diary on a weekly basis where you commit to undertake some form of activity that enables you to remain up to date and connect to the latest developments in the profession and the emerging tools to support delivery of results. Connected to this is your adaptability to change and developing a mindset that enables you to embrace it.

Other people

In some cases it can actually be other people who become professional derailers, sometimes through conscious action but more often through acting in a way which unconsciously impacts on our own behaviour and professional development. Consider a scenario where you are working as part of a team in an organization and you find yourself in the company of an individual or group of individuals who have a somewhat negative attitude towards the work being completed or to the employer. It is a safe assumption that aligning yourself with individuals with such a viewpoint is not going to enable you to achieve the professional results you may otherwise have done. In addition, the reality is that this can occur to varying degrees at all levels of professional competence. For this reason it is important to surround yourself with people who are passionate about your profession and chosen career, and who are therefore more likely to be in a position to enhance and support your career aspirations as opposed to impacting negatively on them.

Influencers and future shapers

In all professions there are individuals who are recognized as influencers and future shapers; people who have an opinion or a vision and who promote it widely in order to build a following and then through that following instigate action and change. There will be some that you relate to and some that you don't. The key point here is to be aware of them and if you find someone who has a vison that resonates with you, align yourself with them so that you can add your voice to help instigate action. Remember that this is in the context of professional development so here we are looking to influencers and future shapers that can be a source of that for you. For that reason, there may be development possibilities that reach beyond the content of the message and information they are sharing. For example, you may find that you learn how to build communities, how to market a product or a service through social media or how to present in an engaging and compelling way on stage. This in turn may then lead you to consider whether becoming an influencer or future shaper is something that you personally aspire to at some point. If it is, this then becomes a professional goal which you should plan in. Determine when you want to have made it happen by, what it will look like for you in terms of the message you want to share, and your unique mix of skills and talents, and then you can map in professional development activities to help you achieve this.

HR leaders

In this chapter I also wanted to consider the changing nature of the HR director role in organizations and establish what this may mean with regard to professional development activity for strategic HR leaders. I interviewed two respected executive search professionals with regard to this.

In considering what skills are currently most in demand from employers looking to hire new HR leaders, Sam Allen notes that employers are requiring their HR lead to have an ability to see the complete business picture and understand their impact on commercials, international experience, digital resourcing experience, and in addition she notes that core skills linked to remuneration, organizational design and industrial relations are still in demand.

When considering what makes a great HR leader stand out from a 'good' one, Sam notes that 'You wouldn't recognize them if they sat around the boardroom table as they are commercial and able to contribute to the overall strategy of the business and its delivery, not just the functional discipline of HR.' An interesting point to note from Sam was that commercial capability is still coming through as a skills gap for HR leaders, particularly in the context of thinking like a CEO.

Orlando Martins expands on this through identifying nine factors that HR leaders need to address in order to transition into a more forward-focused and commercial approach.

- **Managing the internal community**

  Managing communication top down in a digital age is almost impossible. Leaks happen, and social media takes over. To avoid the pitfalls, HR must be the internal movement for a positively engaged community and avoid Glassdoor and social media becoming the forum for the dissatisfied.

  In order to achieve this HR needs to be closely aligned with corporate communications and take advice and technical help from the marketing and brand communication teams.

- **Art meets science**

  The age of human capital and the Victorian factory are dead. High-performing organizations are increasingly using HR analytics to shape their future with the many branches of behavioural science, not least psychology and neuroscience.

  Don't jump for the first tool; be clear about what you are looking for and then shop around.

- **Juggling process, people and structure**

  When it comes to organizational design, too often the focus is on the formal structure and efficiencies, rather than the informal organization and the desired outcomes. To be optimally productive requires HR to have an honest view of their company 'inside out' and then to review and learn the lessons from external markets and in particular direct competitors. That doesn't mean 'cut and paste', it simply provides a base from which to work.

  Specifically designed market intelligence projects are a great way of understanding the inside and outside views.

- **Watching the bench**

  Good football managers always have an outstanding 'bench' and progressive HR directors must be able to identify, assess, develop and protect the best, whilst not being afraid to let underachievers go.

Talent pipelining may be dead but that doesn't stop you continually taking snapshots of the evolving market.

- **Employee motivation**

Recruiting and retaining talent is still the number one challenge for many CEOs but, as organizations are forced to become leaner, HR directors must consider the non-financial motivations when running next year's numbers.

In a time where experiences, free time and training are more valuable than rewards, maybe it is time to consider the bottom line and the feelings that may engender greater loyalty.

- **Where numbers and people collide**

Being on the board requires you to be numerate and develop holistic business cases. If you can't do the numbers yet, we would recommend a strong partner in finance.

If you want to get to board level at any point in the future, find a mentor.

- **Empathy is not just 'tea and sympathy'**

Having a conscience and being empathetic are valuable commodities in a work environment that is increasingly challenged by shifting societal factors. It isn't a return to personnel, it is being human.

If you have become bored of people, or lost heart, it is time to re-engage and remember why you came into HR in the first place.

- **Being digital**

This is not just 'getting things online', it is about a fundamental change in your approach to doing business.

A chat with the CIO/CDO may lead to a winning partnership.

- **Culture, culture, culture**

Often defined by values inscribed on a wall that nobody believes, for tomorrow's leaders companies are going to have to grow into authentic organizations with purpose and a positive culture at heart.

If you don't believe it, nobody will.

Orlando Martins, CEO and Founder, Oresa Executive Search
(www.oresa.co.uk)

Conclusion

A continued focus on professional development is an essential component in being able to operate at a strategic level and delivering results. This starts with building a comprehensive understanding of the various components of the HR profession and then devising mechanisms through which you can keep up to date with emerging trends and developments. It is certainly helpful to look for professional development opportunities that may arise outside of the organization you work in and engage in activities that help you progress and build a reputation in your chosen field. As your career progresses and regardless of the level you attain it is likely that at some point you will encounter potential derailers which you should not ignore. Whilst these cannot always be avoided there are steps you can take to mitigate the impact they have on your professional progress. In addition, it can be a valuable exercise to consider what skills requirements executive search consultants are being briefed on with regards to the lead HR role as they are incredibly well placed to pick up on the frustrations and challenges that CEOs encounter with regard to delivery of the HR role.

Toolkit essentials: 5 steps to accelerate your professional development

1 Start before you're ready: you don't need to wait until everything is perfectly aligned or for a specific moment in time to start taking action with regard to your professional development. The best thing you can do is start to take action today which moves you forward and takes you out of your comfort zone and present sphere of knowledge.

2 Surround yourself with people who are aligned with your career aspirations and who are well placed to inspire, support and motivate you to achieve more.

3 Do your research: read widely across multiple channels in order to really understand the different facets of your profession and remain up to date with emerging trends and developments.

4 Find ways in which you can get involved in activity outside of your current role and organization that will help build and elevate your professional profile and reputation.

5 Establish who are the influencers and future shapers in your profession whose work you feel aligned with and connect with those individuals to help inspire your own learning and development.

Questions for reflection

Q. Which professional derailer are you most at risk from and what steps will you take this week to mitigate it?

Q. Who are the five people who you spend the most time with and do they act as supporters or detractors with regards to your professional development and career ambitions?

Q. What activities could you engage with outside of the organization you work in that would enable you to enhance your professional reputation?

Reference

Carter, C M (2018) Three career development professionals weigh in on the recent rise of job-hopping, *Forbes*, available at: www.forbes.com/sites/christinecarter/2018/07/22/three-career-development-professionals-weigh-in-on-the-recent-rise-of-job-hopping/#66acde662182 [accessed 3 October 2018]

Development of 27
the profession

Introduction

In this chapter we turn our focus to the development of the HR profession and consider emerging trends that are already shaping it. In particular, we look at the shift away from 'Human Resources' as a terminology and explore why more and more HR professionals are moving towards a People Experience (PX) proposition as an alternative. In addition, we also consider the role of all HR professionals in shaping the future of the profession.

How will this chapter shape my thinking?

- It will encourage you to think about your own role in shaping the future of HR.

- It will encourage you to consider alternative delivery models.

- It will prompt you to consider the evolution of the role and what this might mean with regards to skills gaps and sustainability.

Emerging trends

In November 2017, The HR Trend Institute predicted eight major HR trends for the future, which can be summarized as follows (Haak, 2017):

- A switch from a 'please the boss' (PTB) mentality to one of 'employee intimacy' (EI). This move to developing a greater understanding of employee capabilities, wishes and needs is required in order to design more relevant employee journeys.

- A focus on productivity and using analytics to determine the characteristics of the best-performing teams and people.

- A movement towards HR embracing the concept of 'power to the people', where employees are seen to be taking more initiative as a result of being tired of waiting for HR or the organization to take action. Examples include utilizing tech such as WhatsApp and Slack to communicate with teams and individuals as opposed to existing company channels.

- The end of fixed jobs, with teams being made up of individuals who have the required skills for delivery of a specific assignment as opposed to a fixed or siloed role. This leads to less of a requirement for static job names.

- Real-time learning with big chunks of material being divided up to enable micro learning. Learning material also being made available as and when it is required and tailored to the individual needs and requirements of the employee.

- An upgrade of HR operations with a 24/7 focus on hospitality and service for employees within the organization. Utilization of chatbots and high-level professionals to facilitate this.

- A reduction of the number of jobs in HR services as automation replaces manual process, combined with a move to more high-level HR architects with a focus on transforming organizations.

- An approach of 'letting go', where again talent within an organization is encouraged to start initiatives, for example in the field of learning and development, without corporate involvement. The role of HR shifts to one of stimulating such initiatives instead of a focus on trying to control or stop them.

In addition to the above it is also becoming evident that the following are also rapidly becoming hot topics within the HR profession.

Design thinking

In April 2017, Linda Naiman wrote a piece for *Inc.* magazine in which she positioned how design thinking could aid in delivering great employee experiences that served to spark creativity, collaboration and innovation. She observed six trends linking HR and design thinking and connected this with a prediction from Josh Bersin at Deloitte proposing that HR teams will stop designing 'programmes' and instead adopt 'Design-integrated, high-value "experiences" that excite, engage and inspire employees' (Naiman, 2017).

Her article puts forward that HR can leverage design thinking via:

1 Organizational design – by incorporating design thinking in the restructuring of both organizations and individual roles.

2 Engagement – where design thinking is used to make work easier through simplifying processes and making work more rewarding and fulfilling.

3 Learning – in creation of self-directed and user-led learning experiences.

4 Analytics – where data analysis and design thinking are linked in order to deliver solutions directly to the employee

5 HR skills – a key point that HR skills must be upgraded to incorporate capability in 'Digital design, mobile application design, behavioural economics, machine learning, and user experience design'.

6 Digital HR – with regards to the development of new digital tools that make work easier and more effective.

Again we see here how well design thinking integrates with Agile as a working methodology and it is suggested that combining Agile and design thinking in HR will therefore leverage sustained and more commercial results.

It is also important to note that blockchain technology is another emerging trend impacting on the future of HR. The dictionary definition of blockchain is as follows: 'The blockchain is the transaction database linking all computers (nodes) participating and using the

Bitcoin cryptocurrency protocol' (Collinsdictionary.com, 2018). However, where this description relates only to cryptocurrency it is now acknowledged that blockchain will have impact way beyond that, and is already doing so, in particular for HR in the areas of how talent is sourced and verified and also the shape and nature of careers. We will explore this further in the following chapter.

People Experience

In considering the above we can then connect elements of this with our PX model as drawn upon throughout this book and establish how the various components come together in order to deliver results.

A good example of how this approach can operate in practice is demonstrated in the following case study.

CASE STUDY River Island – Nebel Crowhurst,
Head of People Experience

Evolution from traditional HR approached to a People Experience culture

River Island has seen great success, with an established heritage spanning over 70 years. In this time the business and the brand have seen much change and evolution. The retail industry is ever challenged to meet the needs of customers and strong competition means that retailers need to continually be at the forefront of new innovations and product areas. As a family-established and owned business, River Island has a naturally entrepreneurial spirit with an acute awareness of commercial markets and excellent business savvy. In the current economic climate any successful organization knows it need to not only get it right for customers but that it's imperative to also focus on the talent within. Over recent years River Island has exponentially grown its online customer experience with a vision of delivering a seamless shopping experience for our customers between shopping instore and online. This has meant investment in both technology and people. Through this growth the realization that investment in both Customer Experience and People Experience is intrinsically linked, meant the traditional HR function needed to reimagine its approach to supporting business growth.

Traditional HR approaches tend to be detached from business strategy, which negatively impacts the perception people have of what HR can deliver to drive business success. HR functions that are purely transactional tend to be seen as reactive rather than proactive, which results in poor levels of value add and impact. At River Island we wanted to change this and to be recognized as a function that truly makes a difference.

The approach initially required HR to review all its existing working practices and gather insights and feedback from the business on what they felt could be improved. Engaging and listening to people within the organization is key to making the right changes. All too often in HR we think we know all the answers and base our plans on the assumptions we make; unless we proactively spend time talking and listening to people to gather evidence it's impossible to know what changes need to be made.

We soon realized that what was needed was an experience-based approach that gave every person in River Island the sense they were contributing to the overall organizational purpose as well as being made to feel unique and appreciated. Work had already started with creating our Customer Experience map in our marketing team and it was agreed that we needed to somehow mirror this internally by establishing a People Experience map. The idea that we were investing heavily in technology to deliver a seamless shopping experience to our customers made total sense, but what about the experience we were giving our people internally? What did we need to do to invest in this?

Taking a proactive approach to HR and introducing the concept of a People Experience map meant that there was a need to reshape the structure of HR; this has resulted in the introduction of new roles that have a focus on overall organizational culture.

In addition, we needed more effective ways of having two-way communication with our people to ensure we are continually listening to what's working and what's not. Like many organizations we invite our people to contribute to a yearly employee engagement survey, but while this generates useful data for us to make improvements the yearly approach is long and slow. With this in mind the introduction of a new two-way pulse survey means that there is a platform for people to share how they are feeling more regularly; business leaders and functional managers have access to real-time results in a live dashboard, which enables them to respond back to their people and take action much quicker.

For River Island to have a People Experience-based culture we not only needed to reshape the HR function and find more effective ways to listen to people, we also needed to redesign our approach to delivering work. The transformation that is taking place in the growth of technology has been enabled by using Agile methodologies. This is an approach that delivers solutions incrementally, allowing for new ideas to be tested and developed in real time. It empowers teams to be self-organizing and means that the way in which work is prioritized in is in line with the need of the end user (in HR's case, our people). Agile methodologies have historically been perceived to be a set of principles that sit solely within Tech functions, but in recent years other business areas have been experimenting with using some of the core principles to deliver more quickly. At River Island the idea of learning about Agile from our Tech function to enable a more effective flow of work made complete sense. Applying Agile principles into HR at River Island has transformed the way in which we approach large- and small-scale projects, enabling a more proactive approach to supporting the business.

In summary, reimagining the approach to HR into a People Experience culture through the combination of redesigning the HR function, improving the platform of employer voice through two-way pulse surveys and the introduction to Agile methodologies in the workflow has meant a complete shift in the perception of HR in the business. We are being seen as a business enabler that's linked to the overall organizational goals.

Some points to consider for any HR leader keen to make a similar transition:

1 First, an HR rebrand to a new name, whether it be People Experience or similar, is not going to have any impact. Yes of course a new identity may well be needed for HR, but this should come after the groundwork has been done to fully understand the business needs and the structure that's required to sustain growth.

2 This is not an overnight 'quick fix'... it's a long-term cultural change that takes time to embed so you need to be committed.

3 Do what's right for the context of your own organization. While connecting the River Island Customer Experience map to the internal People Experience map and introducing Agile working principles works for us, that may not be the case in other businesses. Don't get swept away with the latest fad or buzzword – do it because it's the right thing to do.

Conclusion

There is much to consider with regards to the development of the HR profession both in terms of how the work will change and how it will be delivered. There are of course no definitive right answers for exactly how the profession will reshape and the beauty of this is that it also means that there are no wrong answers either. For that reason it's safe to say that the future of the profession is in our own hands and every professional working in HR and associated professions today has an equal opportunity to get involved and help shape it. Ultimately, it won't matter what label we put on the work we do, the measure of our impact and the perception of the profession will come from the experiences we curate for businesses and individuals and then how these experiences enable a level of performance that promotes delivery of sustained results.

Toolkit essentials: 5 steps to help you develop a people experience map for your organization

1 Either using a whiteboard or a blank wall and Post-it notes, write out all the events that occur in the employee lifecycle, from pre-hire stage to exit. These events should appear horizontally across the board or wall and will become your PX components; one example of this could be the onboarding process.

2 Then identify a number of 'personas' which represent typical employees at different levels within your business. A persona acts to define an archetypical user of a service or system and is a fictitious example of the kind of person who would interact with it. Start with four or five and then review and refine as you progress with the development of your map.

3 Next, place the information relating to your 'personas' in a vertical line on the left of the board and begin the process of mapping across the experiences each persona requires at each stage of the employee lifecycle journey.

4 When the map is complete, commence a vertical channel review of each PX component. So, in this example you would then isolate 'onboarding' and review the experience requirements vertically across all personas.

5 When this activity is completed for all vertical channels it is then possible to create a backlog of work incorporating these projects and prioritize this in commercial order ready for scheduling and delivery.

Questions for reflection

Q. In what areas of your business is design thinking currently being used?

Q. In what ways could your current HR practices be adjusted in order to nurture fresh thinking and ideas where employees can take ownership of activity traditionally perceived as sitting within the HR remit?

Q. Are there any barriers to deploying new developments in HR in your organization? What would you need to do to overcome these?

References

Collinsdictionary.com (2018) Blockchain: new word suggestion, available at: www.collinsdictionary.com/submission/4349/Blockchain [accessed 8 October 2018]

Haak, T (2017) 8 major HR trends for 2018, *HR Trend Institute*, available at: https://hrtrendinstitute.com/2017/11/27/8-major-hr-trends-for-2018/ [accessed 6 October 2018]

Naiman, L (2017) *Why your HR department should embrace design thinking, Inc.*, available at: www.inc.com/linda-naiman/6-ways-hr-applies-design-thinking-to-deliver-engaging-employee-experiences.html [accessed 8 October 2018]

The future of work

28

Introduction

In this chapter our focus will be on the final pillar of our PX model and we will be exploring themes connected to the future of work. Where it is beyond the remit of this book to offer a deep dive in relation to this particular topic, our aim here is to present prevailing themes in order to promote awareness and curiosity and through that a desire to take action.

> ### How will this chapter shape my thinking?
>
> - It will bring your attention to factors that are already shaping working practices for the future and support you in assessing the potential impact both for yourself and the business you operate in.
> - It will encourage you to consider who is taking ownership for tracking trends in this field within your organization and from that deliver an impact and risk assessment at board level.

The fourth industrial revolution

The fourth industrial revolution, or Industry 4.0 as it is sometimes referred to, encompasses all of the changes emerging in the way we now live, work and communicate, much of this connected to the impact of technology. It is all-encompassing to the extent that it will affect all industries, organizations and professions. One of the primary thought leaders in this area, Klaus Schwab, Founder and Executive Chairman of the World Economic Forum, highlights that dramatic change is now in evidence all around us and that it is happening at exponential speed. Schwab calls for leaders and citizens to 'together shape a future that works for all by putting people first, empowering them and constantly reminding ourselves that all of these new technologies are first and foremost tools made by people for people' (Schwab, 2018).

Indeed, in a feature that appeared on the World Economic Forum's website in June 2017, Brad Keywell, Co-founder and CEO of Uptake, observes that 'The Fourth Industrial Revolution is about empowering people, not the rise of the machines' (Keywell, 2017).

Keywell positions that this empowerment can be achieved by considering the following in relation to adoption of technology and as a response to this incredible pace of change:

- **Mindset.** A repositioning to focus on the fact that new and emerging technology will enable people to become better at their jobs and actually go on to achieve more as opposed to a view that human skills will be devalued.

- **Human and machine.** Consideration that humans and machines both have weaknesses that can be balanced by the other's strengths and where this is achieved people can be empowered to a greater degree than has ever been possible before, with latent creativity and imagination being unlocked at all levels.

- **Power of data, power of people.** Effectively enabling workers on the front line to make decisions, take action and generate solutions directly in order to do their jobs better and create more meaningful work that has a greater commercial impact.

- **New solutions.** Acknowledgement that work can be made easier and delivered more efficiently through the deployment of technologies such as predictive analytics and diagnostics.

- **Virtuous loop.** A reflection that when people and technology work together the work gets done faster, with fewer errors and improved results. This unlocks a degree of productivity that will be broad and deep and span all industries and professions.

Particularly relevant in the context of HR is Keywell's observation that 'Machines will supply us with the insight and the perspective we need to reach solutions. But they won't supply the judgement or the ingenuity. People will' (Keywell, 2017).

Blockchain

As we established in the previous chapter, blockchain can be defined as 'the transaction database linking all computers (nodes) participating and using the Bitcoin cryptocurrency protocol' (Collinsdictionary. com, 2018). However, it is evident that blockchain technology is now influencing a great deal more than cryptocurrency alone and will potentially play a significant role in transforming the world of work.

In this section we draw on the expertise of Andrew Spence, Strategic Workforce Advisor at Glass Bead Consulting and author of the whitepaper 'Blockchain and the Chief Human Resources Officer' (Spence, 2018). He notes that 'Taken to its logical conclusion, blockchain can help us sort out our personal data, allowing frictionless work-matching platforms' and that this challenges existing notions of the job, the firm – let alone HR.'

Spence highlights seven areas where HR leaders can start to focus their attention and recommends the following relevant actions:

- Continue to think broadly about work and how it could be completed, in particular looking at how the business strategy is deployed. This includes automation, outsourcing and a general rethink of the social contract between the employer and workers who support the organization. In particular blockchain offers solutions connected with the verification of employee and potential employee data and the potential to enable solutions to facilitate paying contractors in real time.

- Move from 'jobs' and 'work packages' to 'skills' and 'tasks'. If the thinking is shifted away from set jobs that need to be filled to align more with what tasks need to be completed or sourced it brings a new perspective for talent deployment, costs and organizational design. Acquisition of talent either on a permanent or contract basis is one area in which blockchain has the potential to disrupt, as per our point above..

- Encourage portfolio careers and verified career profiles. This is something that we see happening already with a growing trend for people to adopt portfolio and lifestyle careers where individuals may have multiple sources of part-time income as opposed to being employed full-time by one organization. So here we acknowledge that working patterns may comprise shorter-term contracts in addition to full-time positions for both leaders and workers. A key factor here connected to blockchain is the introduction of digital credentials, also known as open badges.

- Work with technology providers to develop blockchain solutions. To ensure the effectiveness of implementing blockchain solutions in HR it will be essential for HR professionals to actively engage with innovations and developments in this space. This can be done through collaborations, feedback and an open-minded approach with individuals who are happy to experiment and test new technologies as they emerge.

- Get familiar with new blockchain applications and related technologies. Spence notes that 'HR can be a pioneer in the new technology – not just blockchain but also artificial intelligence, robotics, and the Internet of Things, all of which could eliminate some jobs and create new ones.' However, in order for that to happen we need to approach this with a curiosity and proactive mindset in order to become fully conversant in these innovations and role model leadership throughout this transformation.

- Develop a vision for the HR function. Without question, emergence of this technology will change the operating model for HR and in particular the activities that the function conducts. It would be naïve to overlook this and to fail to plan for this eventuality. Spence suggests that 'The HR focus should now be on how to enable self-organizing teams, measure and predict their performance, and ensure that talent systems are effective and fair.'

- Contribute to the development of industry standards. At this moment in time, with regard to the adoption of blockchain, the only certainty we have is that things will change. It's impossible to predict the exact scale and timing of impact. However, what we can do is ensure we keep ourselves and our teams up to date with developments in this area, map across potential impact in the wider business, and ensure we start now to position ourselves with knowledge and leadership as key influencers in the adoption of this technology.

So, at this point in time it is evident that blockchain does indeed have the potential to bring value to HR through benefits including reduction in cost, risk and time to hire. It could radically impact on how talent is sourced and verified in addition to facilitating more organic and lifestyle career models.

In Spence's words it will 'Test the traditional business norms of human resources management', something that all strategic HR professionals need to have on their radar.

The Internet of Things

The Internet of Things is often raised as a key factor influencing the future of work; however, the reality is that it has already been on the radar for a significant time, particularly when we consider pace of change. It is therefore acknowledged that this is no longer an emerging trend but a factor already in existence that is shaping the way we work and live today. Back in 2014, Jacob Morgan described it as 'Simply put... the concept of basically connecting any device with an on and off switch to the Internet (and/or to each other)' (Morgan, 2014). This principle still stands and we are now in a position where we can see this in all aspects of our lives, both at work and at home.

One area of particular interest to HR professionals here is the increase in adoption of technology such as two-way smart speakers and voice-controlled personal assistants. Effectively, with technology such as Siri and Alexa, we all have the potential to become recruiters, trainers and managers of virtual assistants and this now becoming a normal part of life.

Therefore, as adoption of this technology becomes mainstream and more widespread it is essential for us to map across implications and adoption of this both in HR and in the wider workplace. Some factors for HR to consider are as follows:

- **Security**. Data security is still being flagged as a concern with regards to this technology and there is certainly no escaping the fact that the nature of digital virtual assistants is that they are always listening, waiting for the trigger words to activate them. For some, this remains a concern and a barrier to adoption but as with introduction of any new technology it is expected that these concerns will be overcome through evolution of the product, proof of concept that it works over time and evidence of the benefits that can be achieved from deploying it, primarily in relation to convenience and enhancements in productivity.

- **An enabler of performance**. Where a tech-savvy individual has embraced this technology and persisted with it, it is highly likely that their performance at work will improve as a result. This can only be a benefit for employers and a progressive employer would be well placed to support and encourage this. It is, however, acknowledged that in some organizations barriers to adoption in this way will still exist primarily as a result of data security issues as flagged above.

- **A driver of efficiency**. The most obvious example here is that of automated diary management, which completely negates the need for lengthy discussion or e-mail chains when scheduling meetings. If managed effectively technology in this area can record diary activities and schedule meetings and activities through voice commands and deployment of chatbots and AI.

- **A component of experience**. When we consider the experience we are curating for workers within an organization, a key measure is to look for sources of alignment with non-work-related activity. It is still the case that adoption of technology within workplaces still falls behind how we are now deploying technology on a personal level outside of work. This can become a source of frustration and can impact on the perception of the employer in addition to the ability of the individual to perform to their best. Effectively, we need to look for ways to utilize this as an enabler that supports peak performance.

Conclusion

The topic of the future of work is vast and there are many complexities surrounding it. There are also a lot of predictions and assumptions which shape it. It is, however, a key factor which needs to be considered from a strategic HR perspective and certainly from the position of delivering PX within an organization. It's an area that all HR professionals should pay attention to, both for the changes and shifts in working practices that will emerge from it and also in relation to the impact it will have on jobs and careers in HR. It will fundamentally change the way work in our field is completed and therefore the skills that will be required to deliver it.

Toolkit essentials: 5 steps to getting the most from a digital virtual assistant

1 Start with a digital declutter and get your calendar, contact list and files cleaned up as a first step.

2 Make it a habit to use it. The more you do so the quicker you will work through any initial teething issues and move into enhanced productivity.

3 Whichever digital assistant you are using, research tips online relating to it that will help you ensure you are making the most of the functions available.

4 Test out the different elements of functionality and have fun exploring it. For example, look at how you might use it to make restaurant bookings or order products etc.

5 Remember it was created to help make you more productive, to take away stress and to make your life easier. It should act as an enabler of performance for you so if it starts to take up more time in managing it than you gain in enjoying the benefits from it, stop. Review what's going on and start again from point one above.

Questions for reflection

Q. Where is blockchain technology already being deployed in the organization you work in?

Q. What are your personal views on utilizing a digital virtual assistant? How is this shaping your perception of how this technology could be deployed in your organization?

Q. What are the barriers to adopting new technology in your organization?

References

Collinsdictionary.com (2018) Blockchain: new word suggestion, available at: www.collinsdictionary.com/submission/4349/Blockchain [accessed 16 October 2018]

Keywell, B (2017) The Fourth Industrial Revolution is about empowering people, not the rise of the machines, *World Economic Forum*, available at: www.weforum.org/agenda/2017/06/the-fourth-industrial-revolution-is-about-people-not-just-machines/ [accessed 17 October 2018]

Morgan, J (2014) A simple explanation of 'The Internet of Things', *Forbes*, available at: www.forbes.com/sites/jacobmorgan/2014/05/13/simple-explanation-internet-things-that-anyone-can-understand/#59f1c92b1d09 [accessed 17 October 2018]

Schwab, K (2018) *The Fourth Industrial Revolution*, World Economic Forum

Spence, A (2018) Blockchain and the Chief Human Resources Officer: Transforming the HR function and the market for skills, talent, and training, *Glass Bead Consulting*, available at: www.glassbeadconsulting.com/tools-resources-research/blockchain-and-the-chro-report/ [accessed 17 October 2018]

INDEX

Printed in the USA
CPSIA information can be obtained
at www.ICGtesting.com
LVHW071423061224
798379LV00012B/79